THE 3-5-7 MODEL© WORKBOOK

Supporting the Work of Children, Youth and Families Toward Permanency

Developed by Stephanie Hodge Wolfe, MSW
In collaboration with Darla Lynn Henry, PhD, MSW

THE 3-5-7 MODEL© WORKBOOK

Copyright © 2012, by Darla L. Henry & Associates.
Cover Copyright ©, 2012 by Darla L. Henry & Associates.

To order this workbook, contact:

Darla L. Henry and Associates
PO Box 4847
Harrisburg, PA 17111
717-919-6286
ww.darlahenry.org

SECOND SUNBURY PRESS EDITION
Printed in the United States of America
January 2012

ISBN 978-1-934597-78-1

Published by:
Sunbury Press, Inc.
105 S. Market St.
Mechanicsburg, PA   17055

www.sunburypress.com

Mechanicsburg, Pennsylvania   USA

Contents

Purpose of this Workbook

This workbook is designed to provide a beginning set of ideas and activities for professionals working with children and families as they support the important work of children and youth on their journey to actualize permanency. It is intended to support the application of concepts of the 3-5-7 Model© for "readiness to permanency" workers who participate in training and consultation of the 3-5-7 Model©.

The workbook begins with an overview of each of the three tasks of the 3-5-7 Model©. For each of the three tasks, the workbook then provides a practical framework for approaching the work by identifying the key concept, primary questions and suggested activities associated with each task.

Activity descriptions include:

1. Name and purpose of activity
2. List of materials needed
3. Ways to get started
4. Tips and techniques to making the activity meaningful for the youth

Often those helping children, youth and families in their grief and relationship-building work wonder if they are on the right path and often become unsure about what to do next. The answers to their questions become evident the more they understand and use the broader concepts of the 3-5-7 Model©. Following each set of activities are a set of questions to consider. Examining these questions in the context of one's own personal experiences will enhance understanding of the concepts and allow for more success when supporting children, youth and families. Additionally, at the conclusion of the workbook a list of resources is provided that can further the learning surrounding the 3-5-7 Model© concepts.

Introduction

The 3-5-7 Model© is a state-of-the-art, promising practice that supports the work of children, youth and families in grieving their losses and rebuilding their relationships towards the goals of well-being, safety and permanency. It has demonstrated effectiveness as a relational practice to explore with children and youth their feelings about the events of their lives. It is a strengths based approach that empowers the children and youth to engage in grieving and integrating significant relationships. The concepts of the 3-5-7 Model© provide a guided approach to placement preventative and post placement work with children and their families. It is a methodology that can be woven into Family Finding engagement activities and Family Group Decision Making conferences. Practice applications can be made both at intake and throughout ongoing case management services, including protective and placement services that can also support kinship, foster and adoptive family placements. The 3-5-7 Model© provides tools, based on theoretical foundations, to support the work around issues of separation and loss, explore identity formation, establish attachment and relationship building foundations towards permanency, and create feelings of belongingness for the child, youth, and family. In addition, implementation of the 3-5-7 Model© supports deeper therapeutic work around abuse, abandonment and neglect experiences that is or may be provided by other clinical professionals.

The three (3) tasks of the model engage children, youth and families in:

1. **clarification** activities (Life Books, Loss Lines) to identify life events and to engage in grieving opportunities towards reconciling the losses of their lives;
2. **integration** activities (Life Books, collages) to assist them in building and rebuilding relationships through the attachment process; and, in giving meaning to those relationships;
3. **actualization** activities (Life Books, Dream Catcher) to assist them in visualizing future goals and to establish permanent life relationship connections.

The five (5) conceptual questions support the work of the three tasks and address the following:

1. Who am I?: identity formation
2. What happened to me?: separation and loss; the grieving process
3. Where am I going?: attachment cycle as foundation for trust and safety in relationships
4. How will I get there?: relationship building recognizing those who will continue to provide support to them
5. When will I know I belong?: feelings of safety, belongingness and permanency

Throughout the work, as children and youth engage in these tasks, and in answering the five questions, they find the answers to frequently expressed "why" questions will reveal themselves, guiding the planning and decision making process.

Seven (7) skill elements and interpersonal abilities assure the work of professionals and parents:

- to engage,
- to recognize that painful feelings are expressed in behaviors,
- to listen and be present to the expression of feelings,

- to respond briefly as individuals process their thoughts and feelings,
- to affirm child/youth/family perspectives,
- to create perceptions of safety within the helping relationship and environmental settings, and
- to recognize that the work for children, youth and families is to resolve and heal the pain and hurts of the past as a foundation for growth and development.

Doing this work is about the heart of all of us…encouraging the expression of pain and hurt, in a supportive relationship, that connects behaviors to loss and the resultant behaviors that range from sadness/despair/depression to anger and rage. Through the experiences of learning the techniques and theories of the 3-5-7 Model© workers and families become knowledgeable and comfortable in exploring these hurts and in learning patience in supporting the expressions of their pain. As a practice for feelings work, the use of this model has shown that children and youth do the work in grieving losses and are able to move forward towards permanency in relationships.

Use of the 3-5-7 Model© is a practical, doable approach that involves training and consultation for professionals, families and caregivers toward the work of children and youth in their readiness for permanency. It is based in the theories of child development, separation and loss, grief process, family dynamics, impact of abuse and neglect and resilience.

Overview of Clarification, Integration and Actualization

The tasks of clarification, integration and actualization guide our interventions with children, youth and families in working with them towards improving well-being and readiness for permanency. These three (3) tasks provide a method to guide the readiness process. They also indicate where each is in reconciling and grieving losses and in moving toward rebuilding relationships.

Clarification

Essentially, clarification means to identify and make sense out of the events of the one's life, to provide a factual base for understanding and to clarify what is real and what is not real. Clarification is a lengthy process. For children and youth, progress depends on where the child/youth is developmentally and cognitively, as well as their readiness to accept information about their history and life events. This is not a linear process, but one that ebbs and flows. Through clarification, a more defined identity develops and one comes to understand the context of life events, reconciling the losses experienced as a result. As they learn more and remember more about their past experiences, they are supported to safely express painful feelings, love, anger and hatred for others, fears, mistrust, and despair, as well as to more overtly experience a grieving process. When done in the presence of a listening person, on a consistent basis, safety is perceived and eventually trust is felt within that relationship. By remaining present to their grief, the attachment cycle process has continuity and the relationship is strengthened (Fahlberg, 1991).

Integration

Integration is the process by which one develops the ability to understand their connections and membership in numerous families. Many children/youth have lived with a variety of individuals or families before coming into care, and they may have also had several different living situations while in care (foster homes, residential facilities, etc.). Their membership within all these family systems and relationships needs to be explored so they can begin to understand who had meaning for them and for whom they had meaning. As a result, a perspective is gained that they belong to more than one family, enhancing feelings of belongingness and permanency.

During integration, children and youth accept that they do not have to choose membership in a single family. Children and youth begin to deal with loyalty issues toward their biological parents and other relatives if they are not going to return home. Parents come to realize that they have supportive extended family networks. They begin to embrace these relationships and their roles in supporting the parenting of their child.

Actualization

The third task, actualization, is the visualization of permanency; that is, the sense of feeling safe and belonging; claiming an identity; and establishing a place within family or other permanent relationship. Actualization is well-being. It is the ability of the child or youth to begin to see a possible permanent future with a family, parent, or guardian as the tasks of clarification and integration are occurring and evolving. When life events are better understood, when losses have been recognized and are being grieved, when attachments and relationships are identified and continue to be explored, and when identity is more secure, children and youth gain confidence to see the future in relation to reciprocal connections. There is hope for safely becoming a member of a family—whether it is biological, foster, adoptive, kinship, or guardianship —when there is a sense that the potential exists for sharing a common future together. For many children and youth, actualization may be present with several families, similar to extended family relationships inherent in all family structures. In participating in clarification and integration activities, children and youth who are working through the task of actualization make choices based on relational permanency, which may or may not include legal permanency.

The Questions and the Skills

The **5 conceptual questions** guide explorations of the issues of those who have experienced the traumas in their lives that have thrown them off of their developmental courses and unbalanced their homeostasis for growth. The questions are woven into the activities of the three tasks.

- *Who am I?* Identity is formulated by ongoing clarification of life experiences in relation to history, culture, and developmental influences.
- *What happened to me?* Loss experiences are recognized and grieved through clarification of the events that have included separations and abuse events.
- *Where am I going?* Attachments with past and current relationships are integrated through the explorations of the meaning of those relationships. Children and youth begin to make decisions about those with whom they want to maintain a relationship and about those with whom they do not,

even if contact may be limited by safety concerns. These decisions may change through developmental growth.

- *How will I get there?* Repetition of the attachment cycle, with needs being met on a consistent basis, in a stable environment, encouraging relationship building.
- *When will I know I belong?* When a child/youth feels safe and secure in a relationship and families have claimed the child/youth as a family member, the child/youth eventually feels belongingness with the family.

The **7 interpersonal elements** are identified as several of the many skills and values that are needed for those who support the work of youth and families in grieving and relationship building. Critical skills are the ability to:

- **engage** youth and families in activities that explore their lives
- **recognize** that painful feelings are expressed in the behaviors of those who have been traumatized
- **listen** and to be present to the expression of all thoughts and feelings
- **affirm** the pain and hurts from these experiences
- **be present** in order to provide the opportunity for individuals to do the work of grieving their losses and processing their emotions.
- **offer a safe space** for the expression of feelings and exploring thoughts
- **respond briefly** to child/youth efforts to process feelings/thoughts about life events.

Engaging individuals to do the work of grieving and relationship building, using the 3-5-7 Model, requires continuity and stability of caseworker and caregiver support services. The level of trust established during activities, and the overall intensity and duration of the relationship, suggests that the process demands and supplies both emotional and concrete support (Osterling & Hines, 2006). As individuals begin to reconcile their grief, they may more readily enter into deeper, intensive therapies, if needed, through mental health programs, in order to explore the impact that abusive and damaging relationships may have had on them. These 7 skill elements guide the efforts of professionals, counselors, and families as they are present to and support the grief work (Henry & Manning, 2011).

In this description of the elements of the 3-5-7 Model, it is worth noting that the individuals in roles of support should be aware of their own grief processes so that their ongoing grief work will not become barriers to the expressions of feelings and behaviors of the youth who are working through their grief (Henry, 2010). There is no need to be an expert in grieving, but merely to be companions who witness the expressions of others who are experiencing loss, companions who validate and allow the process of grieving to occur (Henry & Manning, 2011).

Important Notes About Applying the 3-5-7 Model

Continuity is critical to supporting the grief process and relationship building works. Children and youth should be seen every other week at a minimum, with phone contact in the interim. This establishes continuity for the work being done and provides the context for a relationship of safety for ongoing expressions of grief (Henry and Manning, 2011).

Use of Activities and Exercises is helpful in engaging those in their grief and loss work. Those supporting the work should be knowledgeable of and have resources to a variety of activities that encourage and support the work of clarification, integration, and actualization, to explore the issues of identity, loss, attachment, and relationship building. Examples of effective activities, although there are many, include: life/loss lines, life maps, collages/puzzles, safety nets, and sand art (Henry, 2005; Jewitt Jarratt, 1982; Keck & Kupecky, 1995; Worden, 1996).

All activities should generally be directed by the child/youth who will demonstrate their comfort level with the exercises through their verbal and non verbal clues. If a child/youth seems uncomfortable, do not push them to do an activity. Be willing to go where the child/youth takes you; possibly with another activity that relates more closely to what the child/youth is expressing at that time.

Life books provide an excellent tool for continuity of the grief process. They provide a tangible and concrete account for the youth of the clarification work that they are doing, as well as a means of reflection between sessions and evidence of the permanency activities that they are exploring (Henry and Manning, 2011).

Those doing this work should have **good communication** skills. Caseworkers have knowledge about abuse and neglect, grief and loss behaviors, adolescent development, and the dynamics of biological and placement families. Effective communication abilities for working within the teams of caseworkers, therapists, and parents are needed. It is critical that workers be comfortable and be secure in comforting the behaviors of grief (Henry and Manning, 2011).

The **power of listening** skills cannot be underestimated. Grief cannot be heard until someone is listening. When we listen to the grief of another, we provide the validation of their being. Most of all, the message they receive is our presence; by being in the moment with them to witness the horrors of their lives, children sense safety and the protectedness that they are not alone as they struggle with the hurt brought into their lives. Listening requires the ability to be silent. Often we feel that we must have answers for the griever to make it better; however, only they can find the answers as they move through their own strengths to find meaning for the loss. Only the one who has experienced the loss can give meaning within their own sense of self. When we emotionally distance ourselves from them and their grief, children often panic and create more extreme behaviors to get our attention to their pain. Making connections will diminish their loneliness and give them hope that someone is there for them to hold them up, listen to them, and protect them from ultimate despair.

Example Applications of the 3-5-7 Model

A worker from California connected a 16-year-old youth with previously unknown family in Virginia after family finding activities were conducted. After training and consultation on the 3-5-7 Model, the worker approached the youth's concerns and apprehensions in the context of his loss feelings and grief behaviors. The youth's ability to understand his feelings and actions in relation to grief behaviors enabled the worker to be present and respond to his reactions of anticipation and uncertainty. Her availability to him to process these feelings provided assurance and the opportunity to clarify his life events of the past so that he was able to conduct a conscious integration of potential new relationships with these current family connections, actualizing permanency in his family relationships (Henry, 2010). While currently not physically living with family in Virginia, he has achieved relational permanency, knowing that he experiences the security of being connected to family through telephone and occasional visit connections (Henry and Manning, 2011).

A permanency specialist used the 3-5-7 Model to prepare a 14-year-old youth in California for reunification with his mother and sister who were living in Wyoming. Reunification with the mother was uncertain as a permanency resource for him since it had been three years since her son had lived with her and they had had limited contact over that time. The specialist and county worker had numerous discussions with the mother by phone to support her concerns, most specifically the grief feelings that she had experienced regarding the situation of her son not living with her. The sister was also included in these discussions regarding loss feelings for her brother. Engaging the youth in a variety of exercises and activities, the specialist guided his work in clarification of his life events, wherein he expressed various feelings related to the losses in his life, and the integration of his family living experiences, giving meaning to numerous relationships, so that he could actualize (envision) the possibility of living again with his mother and sister. Eventually, he made the trip to Wyoming, with a positive reunion outcome. Contact and visitation were continued for several months and reunification resulted when the youth expressed his readiness to return to live with his mother (Henry, 2010).

A supervisor used the concepts of the 3-5-7 Model to help a 12-year-old boy who was experiencing conflicting loyalties for his mother and for his prospective adoptive family. Although willing to be adopted by his foster family, he was not ready to consent to the finalization. He continued to have feelings and thoughts about "leaving his mother" and his concerns for her feelings about his adoption. This creative supervisor decided to allow for contact between the youth and his mother, even though parental rights had been terminated. After two visits, in which the young man was able to find answers to his questions, he was ready to commit to his new family, having actualized his belongingness (feelings of permanency) with them. Using the tasks of clarification and integration, the supervisor had engaged the youth in exploring his understanding of his relationship with his mother, expressing feelings of her loss, and then honoring her presence and ultimately her place in his life. He was able to actualize permanency with his adoptive family by integrating both family relationships in his future (Henry, 2010).

Over series of several meetings with a 10 year old youth, a permanency worker helped youth create a timeline of important events, places where he lived, and important people. The youth drew a picture of his birth home. The permanency worker listened to youth talk about this home, where he was neglected and abused. After the activity, the youth asked the worker to gather photos of his birth home. Reviewing these pictures provided him with an excellent opportunity to discuss how he has taken a journey during his young life, and that he and his brothers are moving toward finding a permanent family. Also discussed was how the youth is now surrounded by adults who care for him and will protect and support him. This youth used the 3-5-7 Model to integrate those experiences, both positive and negative, into the fabric of his life story.

A permanency worker read a book to a school aged youth about a being in foster care. The youth carefully studied the pictures in the book as it was read. The narrative touched on many issues that directly affected the youth, including a parent in jail, a parent who could not provide adequate care, missing his siblings and birth parents, and realizing that being in foster care was not his fault. This validated the youth's feelings and helped the youth feel less isolated and alone.

A permanency worker was working with a family in the process of adopting a teen boy. When he was a very young boy, his birth mother died; his birth father was so grief stricken himself that he shared very little with his son about his birth mother. Her memory sadly became a subject that was not open to discussion. By the use of Family Finding activities, several of the birth mother's family members were found and shared information and pictures of birth mother. This process also prompted birth father and stepmother to pass on to the teen a hand-made stocking that his birth mother had made for him. The teen was so happy to have the stocking he slept with it that night and now keeps it in a special place to honor his birth mother.

A therapist showed an 11-page, computer developed, loss history chart that a 17-year-old youth had completed. The therapist used this activity to support the youth in clarification of the story of his life, identifying the losses within many of these events. The visual history chart helped him in the integration of these events with numerous people with whom he knew and had relationships. As he identified the positives and negatives of these relationships, actualization occurred as he visualized permanency in several of these relationships, desiring to establish more secure connections with them.

Throughout the work to incorporate the 3-5-7 Model in Los Angeles County, whether it was a case-carrying worker who was the person who supported the work or a clinically trained staff member, the result was the same. All reported value in having used the model and noted enhancement in the healing process for the youth with whom they were working. The youth reported that they were able to get in touch with how their experiences had impacted their lives. Having a witness present (worker/therapist), as they re-visited the past with the purpose of making sense of it in the moment, became a corrective emotional experience for them. This was a consistent message from our youth (Henry and Manning, 2011).

Life Books and Life/Loss Lines

Children/youth in foster care are often confused about their identities, their families and their pasts. This confusion is a result of changing caretakers, a scarcity of accurate information, and inadequate preparation for moves. Foster children do not live with people who can verify their pasts, so their confusion continues. Making Life Story Books is one way to reduce confusion. A Life Story Book is a collection of information about a child's life that includes historical data, recollections, memorabilia, and stories by and about the foster child. This organized presentation of the family background and problems, foster care placements, and other life experience provides a child with a clearer picture of his/her life (Beste, 1981). It is also useful in similar work with biological, foster and adoptive families towards their engagement and awareness in grieving their own losses.

The **Life Book** provides a tangible history of the work that is being done by children and families as they attempt to unravel the hurts and confusions of their lives. As it is autobiographical, it reflects their identity development, the reconciliation of losses, and the recognition of connections with significant people and experiences in their lives. By listening to them as they tell their stories, we are able to help them clarify past life events, integrate their relationship experiences, and support the actualization of connections as they continue their life's journey. It is most likely not a quick journey, often requiring many 'tellings' of their stories as they express many feelings about those events. It is a sorting out, a claiming of real emotions, a sense of the found of what may have been lost to them. In doing their work, children and youth are able to find answers that make sense of their experiences. In doing so, they are able to claim their identity and feelings of being valued, increasing their self esteem.

According to those children and youth who have made Life Books, their books are their most treasured possession. The pace is determined by the child/youth doing the Life Book work. Because lack of time has been the most stated reason for not doing life books, the challenge for most Life Book work is just to get started. Most likely it will not be completed; however, the work can be an ongoing process by those who continue to be in contact with the child or youth; and, the child/youth may add to it throughout his/her life.

It is critical, however, that those engaging children and youth in creating Life Books do so on a continuous basis, with at least bi-weekly contact.

Every child, youth or family engaged in grief and relationship building work, should be doing a Life Book. The making of a Life Book should be required, but not be mandated. It is not about the completion of the Life Book, but the doing of it that represents the work that is being done. It reflects the child or youth's practice of clarification, integration and actualization. The book is the possession of the child or youth and should be shared with only those to whom the child or youth gives permission to view it. It is not intended to be a document but a personal account of a child, youth, or family's life.

Youth have reported positive experiences in developing their Life Books. This is an example of what many youth have said:

> *I have started a Life Book and that has helped me tremendously with my self-esteem because I have pictures of all the people that were ever involved with me and that makes me feel that there are people who do truly love and care about me. I was able to make contact with my birth family and stayed in touch with them. At times I have to talk about things that I really don't like talking about. It is really hard stuff to talk about but I learned that there are many reasons to talk about my problems and things that bother me.*

Another effective tool is the use of a **Life Line** or **Loss Line**, a visual representation of each individual's journey through the losses of moves, changes, and relationships of their lives. Vertical and horizontal cross points intersect to indicate where these changes or losses have occurred. They also indicate points where professionals and families have engaged in decision making processes to determine case planning and placement dispositions. The Life Line is a tool for engaging families as it provides information for Family Finding and engagement activities, and for Family Group Decision Making conferences. Developing a Life Line provides opportunities to visually discern all life events in relation to chronological time, thereby, highlighting places for clarification and integration activities towards actualization of permanency.

LOSS/LIFE LINE

Activities at a Glance

KEY:
C = Clarification
I = Integration
A = Actualization

More Activity Ideas

The activities included in this workbook are only a small portion of what can be used in 3-5-7 Model work with children, youth and families. There are many good resources that contain suggestions for activities in which to engage children and youth. Some of the activities that are described in this workbook were gathered by members of the Statewide Adoption and Permanency Network in Pennsylvania. Two additional resources include:

Creative Therapy with Children & Adolescents by Angela Hobday, M.Sh. & Kate Ollier, M. Psych. (1999). This resource includes over 100 activities that can be used in working with children, adolescents, and families.

Creative Interventions for Troubled Children & Youth by Liana Lowenstein, MSW. (1999). This resource provides activities to help children and teens identify feelings, cope with emotional difficulties, strengthen interpersonal skills, and enhance self-esteem. This author has also published additional workbooks that contain activity ideas.

As the worker becomes more familiar with the 3-5-7 Model, adapting activities or creating new activities will come more naturally. An important part of selecting activities to offer children, youth and families is to ensure that the focus of the activity is on clarifying life events and the related feelings, exploring relationships and loyalty through integration of past, current and possible future relationships, and working with feelings and commitments towards the actualization of belonging in a permanent familial relationship.

Activities Related to Clarification

Name of Activity: Life Books

Key Concept: Working with Life Events

Primary Questions: Who Am I?   What Happened to Me?

Purpose: To provide a tangible history of the work that is being done to unravel the hurts and confusions of their lives. The Life Book can include representations that are meaningful from their perspective. Because it is autobiographical, it reflects the work that is being done in reconciling these losses and identifying important relationships in their lives. The Life Book is a tool that gives the worker and the child, youth or family an opportunity to clarify facts, explore feelings, focus on issues of identity and continuity and to integrate past, present and future towards actualizing permanent connections.

Materials Needed: Three ring binder, blank paper, template pages (many suggestions/ideas are available online), markers, crayons, stickers and any other craft items. Photos are also important tools. If there are limited photos, they can be taken as part of Life Book activity work and included.

Getting Started: The most important part of the process is to start by engaging the child/youth/family. Often beginning with topics such as likes and dislikes, interests and hobbies (template pages are helpful for this) allows the individual to begin to get to know you and to begin to feel more comfortable with you. Other ideas include:

- Worksheets that record fun, interesting facts
- For children/youth, what it was like on the day of their birth (current events and other interesting facts about the date of birth can be gather from a simple internet search)
- Constructing family trees
- Recording stories about important people

Information to Obtain from Parents and Caregivers

Many times the developmental and historical information of our children and youth is lost. However, in many cases this information can be recovered simply by asking parents and previous caregivers, whether they are relatives, foster parents or others. The following is a guideline of information that workers can obtain from parents and former/current caregivers:

- Developmental milestones
- Information about injuries, illnesses or hospitalizations
- Favorite activities
- Favorite birthday and Christmas gifts

- The ways child celebrated special holidays
- Favorite friends
- Information about pets in the family
- Information about the ways the child showed feelings/affection
- Pictures of foster family and pets
- Pictures of the foster home
- Pictures of the child with the foster family
- Cute "naughty" behaviors
- Special trips or vacations with the foster family
- Information about reaction and frequency of visits with birth relatives
- Photos of the birth family visiting with the child
- Letters and cards from the birth family
- The child's artwork
- Award certificates, class pictures
- Any special extended family members
- Names of teachers, schools attended, report cards
- Special activities such as scouting, clubs, camping experiences
- Church and Sunday school experiences

Validating the confusion, anger and feelings of the unknown that the child/youth is likely experiencing and will likely bring up, will help them to see you as someone who understands their hurt as a result of being separated from their family Workers can demonstrate this by using the following strategies:

- Act natural, be real
- Ask open-ended questions, avoiding too many specific and direct questions; interact on the child's/youth's level
- Respond in a flexible way, maintaining rapport
- Model feelings, identify them to encourage expression
- Reflect how you feel or felt in a similar situation
- Accept the thoughts and feelings and behaviors that indicate grief stages with a non-judgmental, supportive attitude
- Keep interactions focused on behaviors, perceptions, fantasies and feelings…rather than your own agenda

Tips and techniques to making the activity meaningful: Always leave the child/youth's Life Book in their possession, or with an individual of their choosing. The Life Book is a personal creation. It is not submitted to the agency for the child/youth's record or kept on a shelf out of reach to "protect" it from harm. Some children and youth find it part of the healing process to create and later destroy pages of their Life Books; remember that *painful feelings are expressed in behaviors*, and this is all part of the process. Your role in supporting the work of the Life Book is to follow their lead by offering activities that seem suited to whatever phase of their journey they are currently navigating and to *create a safe space* that provides privacy and is free of distractions. Remember to *keep responses brief*, to avoid getting in the way of their feelings.

Tips for Life Book Activities Based on Child's/Youth's Developmental Level

Preschool and Kindergarten Children: If child is between ages 3 and 6, let him or her do a lot of coloring. You can often help a preschool or kindergarten child make the drawings and speak his story to you. You should act as an interested reporter-secretary, trying to draw your child out while giving encouragement. Write down exactly what he or she has to say. Take your time. Don't insist on the child answering. It may be enough for him to know that you think the topic can be shared.

Middle Childhood: If your child is between ages 6 and 11, allow him to set the pace. Encourage clipping pictures and articles from newspapers and magazines, adding them to the Life Book.

Eleven Years and Older: Most children over age 11 will want to work on the Life Book pretty much on their own, but may need your assistance at times. Be available as a resource for your child or teenager, helping to find information and answering questions.

Name of Activity: Basketball

Key Concept: Working with Life Events

Primary Questions: Who Am I?   What Happened to Me?

Purpose: To facilitate identification and expression of feelings and to normalize that all people experience both positive and negative life events. Modifying the traditional game of basketball can help otherwise reluctant children or youth identify and express their feelings.

Materials needed: Small basketball or some type of round ball, garbage can or something that can function as a basketball hoop, questions (see below), two different colors of index cards or card stock.

Getting Started: Prior to meeting with the child or youth, copy each "Happy Face" question onto one color of the index cards or card stock and draw a happy face on the reverse side of each card. Next copy each "Sad Face" question onto the other color of the index cards or card stock, and draw a sad face on the reverse side of each card. Explain to the child that you are going to play a special kind of basketball, which will help them to discuss happy and sad feelings.

The child/youth attempts to throw the ball through the hoop. If the child/youth is successful, he/she picks a card from the "happy face" pile. These questions relate to happy experiences in a person's life. If the shot is unsuccessful, a card is selected from the "sad face" pile. These questions relate to unhappy experiences. The child/youth can choose to answer that question, pass, or ask for help. The game can continue until all of the questions have been answered or until a pre-determined period of time has elapsed. The worker may wish to stop the game periodically to reflect on feelings or issues disclosed by the child/youth. Remember to provide the option for the child/youth to decline questions that they do not feel ready to discuss. This will allow the child/youth to share information at a pace that feels safe and comfortable.

Happy Face Cards:

- Tell about the happiest moment of your life.
- Tell about a happy memory you have from when you were very little.
- Tell about a time someone did something nice for you.
- Tell about a time you and your family did something fun together.
- Tell about a good dream you had.
- What's the best thing that's happened to you this week?
- Tell about something you have accomplished.
- Tell about a time you did something brave.
- Tell about something that makes you laugh.
- Tell about a time you were able to solve a problem you had.

Sad Face Cards:

- Tell about a sad moment in your life.
- What would you say to a child who was smiling all the time, when you know he is really sad?
- What is your biggest worry?

- Tell about a bad dream that you had.
- Tell about a time someone did something that upset you.
- When was the last time you cried? What happened that made you so upset?
- Tell about a problem you are having at school.
- Tell about a problem you are having at home.
- Tell about a problem you had this week.
- What is something you would like to work on or improve about yourself?

Tips and techniques to making the activity meaningful: This is an activity that could also be used in a group setting. In groups, each child/youth takes turns shooting a basket and answering the questions. In a group setting, experiences can be normalized and validated by asking questions such as, "Has this happened to anyone else here?", "Who else has felt this way?", or "What do others in the group think about what was just said?".

This activity originates from *Creative Interventions for Troubled Children & Youth*, by Liana Lowenstein, MSW. Lowenstein, Lianna. (2006). Creative Intervention for Troubled Children & Youth. Champion Press, Canada. The author has also published other similar workbooks that could provide additional activity ideas.

Notes/Adaptations:

Name of Activity: Bull's-eye Feelings

Key Concept: Working with Life Events

Primary Questions: Who Am I?   What Happened to Me?

Purpose: To provide an opportunity to re-visit the child/youth's feelings related to various life experiences.

Materials needed: Bull's-eye template with four different colored rings to represent four basic feelings, small foam shapes (from craft store) or small pieces of construction paper, tape, and markers

Getting Started: Begin the activity by reviewing these four basic feelings: happy, sad, scared, and angry. Depending on the child/youth's age, ask them to make facial expressions to represent these feelings. Often times, children enjoy seeing their own expressions, so a small mirror or digital camera would allow them to view their own expressions as these feelings are being discussed.

For younger children, come prepared with "losses" that the child has experienced written on the small foam shapes or slips of paper (i.e. moving to a new foster home, changing schools, separation from siblings, making new friends). Some of the foam shapes/slips of paper should also include positive experiences (i.e. vacation with the foster family, reunification with birth family, visiting with a former foster parent). For older children/youth, you may want to brainstorm the losses and changes together and allow the child to write these onto the shapes themselves.

Spread the shapes out on the table and allow the child/youth to choose whichever shape he or she desires to begin with. Have the bull's-eye template posted across the room and encourage the child/youth walk quickly to the bull's-eye and tape the shape into the corresponding color coded feeling ring. Proceed to encourage the child to place the shapes onto the corresponding feeling rings. After all of the shapes have been taped onto the bull's-eye, take the time to reflect on the experiences that the child has encountered. Are many of the items placed in the angry ring? In the scared ring? Discuss what this means for the child and how can they grow from their past experiences. Emphasize and encourage the positives.

Tips and techniques to making the activity meaningful: It may be beneficial to complete this activity once the child/youth and worker have discussed some of the significant changes that have taken place.

Notes/Adaptations:

Name of Activity: Feelings

Key Concept: Working with Life Events

Primary Questions: Who Am I?   What Happened to Me?

Purpose: This activity provides the child/youth with an opportunity to describe her feelings about certain events in their life.

Materials Needed: Digital camera, markers/colored pencils/crayons, pages for Lifebook with the following titles: Things That Make Me Happy, Things That Make Me Sad, Things that make me Scared, Things that make me Angry.

Getting Started: Offer child/youth the opportunity to talk about feelings. Ask the child/youth to name different types of feelings. As the child names feelings words, write them down. If the child decides to talk about any particular feeling, follow this lead. If not, focus on the feelings of happy, sad, angry, and scared. Ask the child /youth to show you by her facial expression what each of these feelings looks like so you can take photos of the feelings. You can also ask the child/youth to choose some feelings to "act out" (in a safe manner).

Discuss the feelings of happy, sad, angry, and scared in depth. Ask the child/youth to list times when he/she felt each of the four feelings (depending on the age of the child/youth, you may have them write the list on the page, draw pictures, or tell you so you can write the list).

After the photos are printed, they can be added to the Lifebook.

Tips and techniques to making the activity meaningful: This activity can be completed once the worker has met with the child/youth several times and has established a relationship with the child/youth. This activity can be used for most ages. You will likely need at least an hour, possibly more depending on the child's level of understanding.

Notes/Adaptations:

Name of Activity: Feelings Tic Tac Toe

Key Concept: Working with Life Events

Primary Questions: Who Am I?   What Happened to Me?

Purpose: To identify and express feelings related to being in foster care. To help prompt the child to talk about how they are feeling about an upcoming event, such as a pending adoption, reunification with birth family, or a traumatic historical event, such as the death of a loved one.

Materials Needed: Feelings Tic Tac Toe worksheet (Tic Tac Toe grid with pictures that represent the following feelings in each square: happy, mad, nervous, scared, loved, guilty, jealous, sad, relieved; or you can use other feelings on the grid as well). Wrapped candy pieces for markers on the game card.

Getting Started: Players alternately place their candy pieces on the work/game sheet provided in an attempt to get either an uninterrupted horizontal, vertical, or diagonal line of three.   Once a player places a line of three candies, he must uncover the feelings faces in the line and describe a time when he experienced each of those three feelings. If he talks about all three feelings, he gets a point. If no player gets a straight line, nobody gets a point for that round. Once a player accumulates five points, he gets to eat one of the candies. This game of Tic Tac Toe can be used with an individual child/youth playing with the worker, or it can be used in pairs of children/youth of similar levels of functioning.

Tips and techniques to making the activity meaningful: Most children/youth are familiar with the game of Tic Tac Toe and will enjoy this version of the game. Children are generally able to understand the concept of feeling happy, sad, or mad. Other feelings, such as guilt or jealousy, need to be explained using examples that the child will understand. For example, "Guilty means feeling bad about what you did. If you cheat on a test, you would feel guilty when you realize that you did something wrong." Once the child comprehends each of the feelings on the game board, he is better able to ascribe feelings to situations in his own life. As the child talks about his feelings, the worker can reflect on the child's feelings, ask the child to elaborate, and praise the child for his openness. When it is the worker's turn to share, the worker can tailor responses in a way that would be beneficial to the child. This activity is best completed when the worker has a good relationship with the child and knows the child's history and current situation.

This activity originates from *Creative Interventions for Troubled Children & Youth*, by Liana Lowenstein, MSW. Lowenstein, Lianna. (2006). Creative Intervention for Troubled Children & Youth. Champion Press, Canada. The author has also published other similar workbooks that could provide additional activity ideas.

Notes/Adaptations:

Name of Activity: Getting to Know You

Key Concept: Working with Life Events

Primary Questions: Who Am I?   What Happened to Me?

Purpose: To help child/youth identify her favorites, likes, dislikes, thoughts about her family, future dreams, and so on. This can be a great way to start to get to know a child/youth, making it a good warm up or introductory activity.

Materials needed: Prepare a plastic ball (approximately 8 inches in diameter) in advance with questions written on it. Some ideas include:

- What is your date of birth?
- What is your middle name?
- What activities do you participate in?
- What is your favorite season?
- What is your favorite holiday?
- What is your favorite song?
- Who is someone you like to spend time with?
- If you were an animal, what animal would you be?
- Where is a place you would like to visit?
- If you could have a superpower, what would it to be?
- If you could change something about yourself, what would it be?
- If you could be someone else for a day, who would you be?
- Who is someone you care about?
- What is your favorite memory of your mother?
- What is your favorite memory of your father?
- What is your favorite memory about siblings?
- What is a favorite family tradition?
- Who do you talk to when you are upset or mad?

Getting Started: Stand across from the child/youth (if worker and child/youth are playing alone) or stand in a circle if there are multiple players (siblings or same aged peers). Explain that the ball will be tossed or passed back and forth. Ask that the child/youth answer the question that her right thumb lands on. A variation for multiple participants could be that the person to their right or left must answer the question.

Tips and techniques to making the activity meaningful: This activity can be tailored to many topics, depending on the questions selected for the ball.

Notes/Adaptations:

Name of Activity: Grief and Loss Jenga

Key Concept: Working with Life Events

Primary Questions: Who Am I?   What Happened to Me?

Purpose: To open a dialogue regarding child/youth's past experiences. Also initiates questions related to separation and loss which can facilitate discussion about adoption, birth family members and life experiences.

Materials Needed: Jenga game, questions listed on index cards

1. Name someone in your family and talk about something you like about them.
2. If you could change one thing about yourself, what would it be?
3. What do you like about yourself?
4. What are you afraid of?
5. What is your favorite color?
6. What is your best quality?
7. What is one thing you do when you are angry?
8. What is one thing you do when you are sad?
9. Tell about a happy memory you have.
10. Tell something that you like about your family.
11. If you could change one thing about your family, what would it be?
12. Name someone you admire and explain why.
13. What is your favorite food?
14. Tell about a time you felt excited.
15. Tell about a time you felt angry.
16. What is one thing you do not like?
17. Name three nice things that you can do for someone.
18. Where do you see yourself in one year?
19. Where do you see yourself in ten years?
20. If you had three wishes, what would they be?
21. What is one thing you like about your body?
22. What are three things you like about yourself (inside)?
23. What is one thing to say when you meet a new person?
24. What are two things not to do in school?
25. What is one positive thing about school?
26. Name two good things to eat for breakfast.
27. What are two activities to do after school (other than homework and chores)?
28. What is a chore that you don't mind doing?
29. Name one teacher you liked and explain why.
30. Demonstrate a positive facial expression for meeting someone.
31. Demonstrate how to greet someone you haven't seen in a few months.
32. Describe what you expect this school year to be like.
33. What is your favorite subject?
34. Name one good thing that happened last week.
35. What is one hope that you have for your future?

Getting Started: Set up the game as normal. When each player chooses a tile from the tower, he/she selects a card and reads the question on the card. Question should be answered prior to placing the tile on the top of the tower. A player can pass a question if he/she chooses. If a player continues to pass on questions, at the end of the session, discuss with him/her the reasons why they chose not to answer the question(s).

Tips and techniques to making the activity meaningful: A variation of this activity is to explain to the child/youth that each of you will take a turn removing a block from the tower. Before removing a block, the player must name something that a family does for each other. Take turns naming family responsibilities and removing blocks from the tower until the tower falls. When the tower falls, ask the child/youth to imagine that each block that was removed from the tower was something that a family does for each other. Then ask the child/youth what happens when family members stop doing these things for each other. If the child/youth is hesitant or not sure, prompt them by asking them what happened to the tower when the blocks were taken out. This is helpful in starting a dialog about reasons that children come into foster care. Once you've started a discussion about reasons children come into foster care, give the child/youth a piece of paper or cardstock and ask them to think of some reasons they are in foster care. Because many children/youth are hesitant when it comes to this subject, it helps to let them know that you already know the reasons that they came into care and that it is your job to help make sure that they know information related to their removal. You can also assure them that you will not make them talk about things they do not want to talk about.

Notes/Adaptations:

Name of Activity: I Am a Bouncy Ball

Key Concept: Working with Life Events

Primary Questions: Who Am I?   What Happened to Me?

Purpose: To illustrate how the child/youth/family is resilient; to provide a sense of hope for the future.

Materials Needed: Bouncy ball

Getting Started: Show a bouncy ball, like one you can get out of a machine at the grocery store. Ask what the individual thinks they have in common with the ball. Inform the individual that they are more like the ball than they think – and it a wonderful thing.

For children, talk about how they came into foster care, all of their moves "bouncing from foster home to foster home," and about some of the difficult experiences they have had. Give the ball a good throw so that it bounces off of the floors/walls/other objects in the room. Explain that the ball was "bouncing all over" from place to place, is having a hard time settling down (the ball just keeps bouncing and rolling), will sometimes get itself "lost" under the couch or chair, and is sometimes forgotten. Point out that this may be how the youth has felt at times. Next pick up the ball and step on it, try to squish it and try to twist in it half. Explain that nothing breaks the ball. Suggest that the ball is the youth. Explain that even after all the bouncing around, the "trauma" of trying to break it or damage it, the ball is still smooth and round and intact. It looks the same, even though it has been through a pretty tough time. Explain that like the ball, the youth too has been bounced around, people along the way may have tried to hurt him, he has probably felt "lost" at one time or another and maybe even forgotten. Suggest that the child is like the bouncy ball and can make it through this awful stuff and be destined to do great things.

For parents you might discuss challenges with parenting and provision of care and safety for their child; personal challenges and experiences could also be discussed.

Tips and techniques to making the activity meaningful:

Helping individuals to see that no matter what they have faced, they have unique strengths and can move forward. This is an important part of being able to cope with the separations and losses they have experienced. Each separation and each loss is an exercise for the child/youth/family in the perception of a "safe" environment in which to do their grief work. Resilient individuals develop coping skills that need to be recognized as such, rather than being labeled as challenging behaviors (Henry, 1999).

Notes/Adaptations:

Name of Activity: Life Map

Key Concept: Working with Life Events

Primary Questions: Who Am I?   What Happened to Me?

Purpose: A Life Map is a visual tool that can be used for a variety of purposes, including:

- to facilitate communication about the past (real or virtual),
- to find out and talk about how the individual perceives and feels about various events, relationships, significant others, time frames and lapses, etc. in his/her life experience (real or virtual)
- to help understand the degree of significance, of often times scanty and scattered pieces, of information obtained about one's life, birth family, past foster families, pets, etc. and,
- to help understand and interpret the various pieces of information that he/she has obtained about his/her life circumstances (Keck and Kupecky, 1995).

Materials Needed: Paper, markers, crayons, pencils, colorful stickers representing life events, people, and places.

Getting Started: Start off with the day they were born. Choose a sticker or create a small drawing at the corner of the page to represent that day. Some might be comfortable with your invitation to begin drawing a map that reflects their life by starting at whatever point in time they are currently when doing this activity.

Next, following their lead, ask them to talk with you about the important events in their lives, allowing them to direct the conversation and creating a representation of each event on the page in the form of a path. Allow them to share as much or as little as they like about each event, being careful not to move too quickly. The idea is to allow them to feel the emotions of the event, so ***keep your responses brief*** and supportive, ***affirming painful and hurtful experiences*** along the way.

Tips and techniques to making the activity meaningful: Avoid the temptation to correct information that is provided. If you have additional information to offer, let her know and ask if she would like to hear the information you have. The worker's role is to provide any additional factual information, but remember that the purpose of the Life Map is for the individual to tell the story from her perspective. It is her work to make sense of it all, and to begin the process of integrating it into a framework of relationships that makes sense to her. The Life Map becomes the story of her life from her point of view. What events in life are remembered? Which events had an impact on her? The ***ability to listen*** is critical to the success of this activity.

Notes/Adaptations:

Life Map

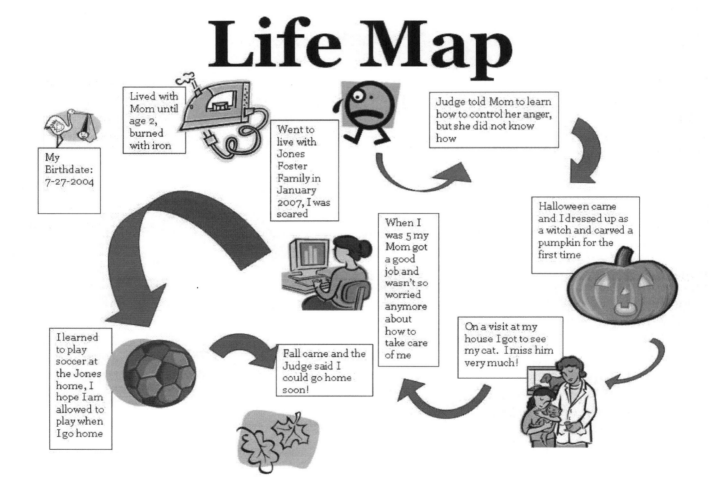

My Birthdate: 7-27-2004

Lived with Mom until age 2, burned with iron

Went to live with Jones Foster Family in January 2007, I was scared

Judge told Mom to learn how to control her anger, but she did not know how

Halloween came and I dressed up as a witch and carved a pumpkin for the first time

When I was 5 my Mom got a good job and wasn't so worried anymore about how to take care of me

On a visit at my house I got to see my cat. I miss him very much!

I learned to play soccer at the Jones home, I hope I am allowed to play when I go home

Fall came and the Judge said I could go home soon!

Name of Activity: Loss History Chart

Key Concept: Working with Life Events

Primary Questions: Who Am I?   What Happened to Me?

Purpose: To identify loss experiences and how the individual was supported/comforted in his grief. It identifies the loss, when it occurred, what was said or done by others when the loss occurred, and the feelings/thoughts about the loss. This tool provides a chronological record of losses. It also provides an overview of what support was given when the child/youth experienced a loss.

Materials Needed: Sheet of 8x11 paper, writing tool. Those familiar with computers, may chose to do their chart on the computer. Divide the paper into five columns: age at time of loss; type of loss; circumstances of loss; help given; and, effects on child/youth/family.

Getting Started: Ask about a time when they lost someone or something. This will begin a discussion about what happened, when and who was there. This discussion can then include feelings about these events. The worker engaging individuals in this activity can put this information on the chart as the conversation unfolds. At any point, the child, youth or family may chose to enter the information themselves.

Tips and techniques to making the activity meaningful: Be patient. This tool supports the recognition of loss experiences and each event may require time for the processing of feelings and thoughts. It is most important to listen and affirm these expressions. The chart may be used over a period of time and numerous sessions with the child/youth/family.

Notes/Adaptations:

Name of Activity: My Life Soundtrack

Key Concept: Working with Life Events

Primary Questions: Who Am I?   What Happened to Me?

Purpose: The primary focus of this activity is to help children use music and musical lyrics as a way to identify and connect with others, and appropriately express their emotions. The activity can be elaborated for musically creative children.

Materials Needed: Create a *My Life Soundtrack* worksheet with the following headings:

- My theme song is…
- I chose this song because:
- A song that makes me happy is:
- A song that makes me sad is:
- A song that helps me release my anger is:
- A song that I can relate to is:
- My favorite song is…and this is why:
- This song creates a lot of feeling when I listen to it:
- This song reminds me of a particular event in my past is…The event was:
- My favorite style of music is…and this is why:

Getting Started: The child/youth should be presented with *My Life Soundtrack* worksheet. The worksheet can be given to the child during the prior session, in order to give the child more time to think of their responses. If it is presented during the session in which the worker intends to complete the activity, expect to give the child more time to think about their responses. The worker should begin talking with the child about the emotional connection that singers have to the songs they sing. Talk to the child about the emotions they feel listening to the song. Suggest they pretend to be a song writer and ask the child to share what life experiences they may choose to write about. Each response the child gives on the worksheet should be processed with the child to gain a better understanding of the emotions that the child is experiencing and how they are managing those emotions. Sometimes, the child can provide specific lyrics to the songs they chose, which can be processed with the child. If the child does not know the lyrics, the worker can extend the activity by printing out the lyrics for the child and processing those specific lyrics with the child during the next session.

Tips and techniques to making the activity meaningful: A CD with the child/youth's chosen songs on it can be made and given to the child, or an i-Tunes gift card can be purchased for the child/youth so that songs of their choice can be purchased.

Notes/Adaptations:

Name of Activity: Oh, The Places I've Been

Key Concept: Working with Life Events

Primary Questions: Who Am I?   What Happened to Me?

Purpose: Visiting significant places can help the child to answer "Who am I?" by giving him pieces of his history, and validating this history as a part of who he is. It also addresses the question, "What Happened to Me?" by retracing the child/youth's steps and revisiting significant places; literally looking at what happened to this child. This is an activity that can be used alone or in conjunction with the *People I've Known* activity.

Materials needed: Camera for video and/or photographs, child/youth placement history (including exact locations), addresses of therapists' offices, schools, child welfare offices, daycare, and so on, paper, markers, crayons, pens, glue/tape, stickers and crafts for decorating Lifebook pages.

Getting Started: Look through the child/youth's case records for information regarding placement history. If a Timeline and/or Life Map have already been completed, these can be used as a reference. Next take the child/youth to visit each of these places. Talk with the child/youth about each placement. Invite the child/youth to talk about their memories at each of their former homes - who lived there, what they liked/didn't like about it, what school was like, what they remember about leaving, and any other information the child/youth remembers. The child/youth's thoughts can be recorded in the Lifebook. If possible, take pictures or video while visiting each location.

This activity can be done at the same time as the *People I've Known* activity. It can be done with any significant places in the child's life. This can include: birth homes, foster homes, group homes, residential treatment facilities, therapists offices, doctor's offices, schools and daycare centers, favorite play spots, court, child welfare agency offices, vacation spots, sports fields, homes of relatives and friends, and the hospital where the child was born. A variation of the activity can be completed as well, *Places to Go*, that includes significant places in the child's life where they have not been before, such as grave sites, the place where his parents met, got married, grew up, or went to school.

Tips and techniques to making the activity meaningful: The child will need a great deal of support to work through issues of separation and loss that may become fresh after revisiting these places and his past. For most children and youth, while this experience raises a lot of separation and loss issues initially, with the help of supportive adults, the experience is ultimately one of healing.

Notes/Adaptations:

Name of Activity: People Who Care About Me

Key Concept: Working with Life Events

Primary Questions: Who Am I?   What Happened to Me?

Purpose: To help the child/youth see that there are people in his life who care about him and to identify people who have contributed to the child/youth's life in the past by supporting and nurturing him. Discussing how these people have or could help the child, can address the question "How Will I get There?"

Materials Needed: Pens, markers, crayons, paper, camera (optional), crafts and decorations like stickers and stencils

Getting Started: Begin by talking with the child/youth about how everyone has people in their lives who care about them. Ask the child/youth to help you brainstorm the names of people in his life who care about him. The child/youth may be resistant to this at first; some children and youth do not feel like anyone cares about them. Give suggestions if needed, including birth family members, previous foster parents, siblings, caseworkers, therapists, teachers, neighbors, friends, and others. Then, have the child tell you how he knows this person cares. Some children will think only of concrete things like "They give me presents." Prompt the child to consider other, less obvious ways that people show that they care. Parents, for example, may make you eat vegetables or go to bed on time because they care about you. After identifying the people, use the paper and pens to make a list, possibly making individual pages for each person. The paper should identify the name of the person, how the child knows that person, and how the child knows the person cares about him. In addition, to address the question "How will I get There?" you can have the child identify how the person can or has helped them throughout their journey.

Tips and techniques to making the activity meaningful: Follow the child's lead of how creative they want to be. Help the child decorate the pages with stickers, stencils, and glitter. If possible, take a photograph of the child with each person for use with this activity.

Notes/Adaptations:

Name of Activity: Safety Quilt

Key Concept: Working with Life Events

Primary Questions: Who Am I?   What Happened to Me?

Purpose: To explore the importance of safety and the feelings associated with safety.

Materials Needed: *Kids Need to Be Safe* book by Julie Nelson (or any other book about foster care/being safe could work), card stock, 8-15 pieces (depending on size) of colorful paper cut so that they could be made into a "Quilt", and a bed template to glue the quilt pieces onto.

Getting Started: Read the book with the child. If they can read, let them read it to you. Then have the child pick pieces of paper and identify what makes them feel safe in their placement or who the child feels safe with (alter to each child's specific situation). Assist the child in gluing each piece of paper onto the bed template. Write what the child says either on that particular quilt piece (depending on size) or on a separate piece of paper. As the child is placing the pieces of the quilt onto the bed, discuss the importance of feeling safe in a home. In order to rest peacefully the feeling of safety and security must be present. There are many ways to be creative with this activity. You could create many different types of quilts such as a feelings quilt, family quilt, or a future quilt.

Tips and techniques to making the activity meaningful: This activity is useful at the beginning stages of out-of-home placements, as way to begin conversation with the child regarding the reason for their removal from the home.

Notes/Adaptations:

Name of Activity: Self Pillow

Key Concept: Working with Life Events

Primary Questions: Who Am I?   What Happened to Me?

Purpose: Provides a tangible representation of the child/youth to honor all that makes up who he/she is.

Materials Needed: 12 square pieces of different material (5" square), 1 rectangular piece of material (approximately 14" x 18"), batting or fiber fill, scissors

Getting Started: Have the child/youth choose 13 different fabrics which represent aspects of who she is. For example, a Strawberry Shortcake fabric may represent a child-like side of the child/youth. Fabric with lightening on it could represent an angry side. Green and red plaid might represent an organized/neat side. You will need approximately ¼ yard of each fabric except the backing fabric which needs to be approximately ½ to ¾ yard of fabric.

Have the youth cut 5" x 5" squares out of 12 different fabrics and the last fabric should be approximately 14" x 18". If you don't sew, find someone who is willing to sew the pillow together for you (leaving an opening so the youth can stuff the pillow). You can also sew it so the seams are on the outside and allow the fabric to fray after washing.

Tips and techniques to making the activity meaningful: Discussions focused on how people tend to put us in "boxes" and identify us as just one part of ourselves. For example, the teenager is a trouble maker or she is an angry person. However, this is not the whole picture of individual; all people have positive and negative sides to them. Every person is made up of many parts which makes the whole individual. This can also be transferred to how the client may also identify others by just one part and how she needs to look at others as made up of different parts, both positive and negative. If you sew the seams on the outside and then wash it, the edges fray. Discussions can then focus on how every person has "rough edges", but as we grow, those rough edges often make us stronger. The person they are today, especially in regard to how they handle/cope with their negative feelings, such as anger, does not have to define who they will become in the future.

Blank puzzle pieces can also be used and the child/youth can decorate each puzzle piece to describe a part of them. Blank puzzles can be purchased at many craft stores.

Notes/Adaptations:

Name of Activity: Sibling Memories

Key Concept: Working with Life Events

Primary Questions: Who Am I?   What Happened to Me?

Purpose: To recognize and value siblings as an integral part of identity development, and to honor the memories of siblings.

Materials Needed: Camera, video recorder, audio recorder, photos, craft pens and pencils, glue, border prints, paper, scissors

Getting Started: Invite the child/youth to talk about his siblings. Ask the child/youth to recall the memories of his brothers and sisters. Record the specific memories as stories that can be made into a collection for the child's Lifebook. The child/youth may choose to make collages of the things that the children like to do together, of the things that the sibling likes most, or of the things that remind this child of their sibling(s). Take photos of the child during visits with his siblings and maintain them as part of the Lifebook. Let the child/youth participate in having duplicate photos made to send to siblings. Schedule opportunities when possible to have siblings visit and plan ahead to have each child/youth share a few of his or her most predominant memories of his siblings. You can videotape or audiotape these stories so that each child will be able to hear the stories over and over again.

Tips and techniques to making the activity meaningful: As you discuss and record the memories in whatever way the child/youth has chosen, be sure to help the child/youth draw connections between himself and his siblings. Help him to see the similarities and the differences to help him build self-esteem and a stronger sense of self-awareness. Be aware of and prepared to process not only happy memories, but also those less pleasant memories that might be brought up. Ultimately, it is all of the memories that will help him to form a most complete picture of who he is and what has happened to him. Don't forget that siblings created through any out of home placement, although not genetically related, are still sometimes siblings with whom great connections have formed and these relationships should also be recognized.

Notes/Adaptations:

Name of Activity: Silhouette

Key Concept: Working with Life Events

Primary Questions: Who Am I?   What Happened to Me?

Purpose: To help the child/youth honor the qualities of birth family members and to discover what traits he carries on from his birth family.

Materials Needed: Light (flashlight, lamp, or light from a video camera) to shine and cause a shadow on a flat surface, black or white paper, pencils, pens, crayons, markers, gel pens, information and or/pictures of birth family's physical characteristics and personalities/abilities.

Getting Started: Use the light to project a shadow of the child's head and upper torso onto a piece of paper that is fastened to a flat wall surface. Trace the outline of the child onto the paper with a pen or pencil. When complete, remove the outline paper from the wall and move to a table with your pens, crayons, gel pens, and markers. With the help of the child, write examples of characteristics that the child gets from her birth family directly onto the silhouette. Example: "I get my blue eyes from my Birth Mother." or "I am good at playing baseball, like my Uncle Charlie." Anything that the child remembers should be on the silhouette.

Tips and techniques to making the activity meaningful: Discussion about all types of birth family information are likely to arise from this exercise as are questions about what the child might have inherited from her birth family's characteristics and abilities. Be prepared to listen to the child's pain and to write down questions that you and the child can later investigate together.

Notes/Adaptations:

Transfer of Learning

Consider the following questions to enhance your understanding of the task of Clarification:

Recall a time when you were in an unfamiliar place and you did not know your way. What did it feel like when you first realized you were lost? How did you find your way? Did you ask for help? If so, how did you choose whom to ask? What feelings did you experience when you knew you were headed in the right direction?

Think of a time when you were overwhelmed by news of some kind (tragic event in the world, diagnosis of your own serious illness or serious illness of a loved one). What information did you seek? How did it feel to have answers to your questions?

Recall a time when you and a family member saw something very differently. How was it that your perceptions of the same event were so different? Was one of you wrong? Why or why not?

Activities Related to Integration

Name of Activity: Candle Lighting Ceremony

Key Concept: Working with Family Relationships and Loyalty

Primary Questions: Where Am I Going? How Will I Get There?

Purpose: To recognize, remember, and honor those who have impacted the child or youth; to give symbolic meaning to memories of significant relationships and expressions of lost persons; to provide significance to experiences that hold special value.

Materials Needed: Candles/candle holders to represent each of the people listed below, lighter/matches.

Getting Started: This activity is best suggested prior to the time that you wish to hold the ceremony, so that the child or youth will have time to prepare for their participation. The worker can start by simply stating that candles will be lit as a remembrance of those people who have impacted her life.

1. The first candle is for our birth parents. We light it in honor of the gift they gave us ~ the gift of life.

2. The second candle is to remember our foster parents ~ the people who cared for us on our journey.

3. The third candle is for the memories that were especially hard for us. This candle is for thinking about those adults who should have cared for us but didn't. Maybe they hurt us. The light reminds us that we are going to be able to look at sad memories, too. They are part of the past.

4. The fourth candle is for the people we had to leave behind ~ perhaps a grandparent or a birth sibling. These are sometimes sad memories, too. The light reminds us that we are getting strong enough to look at those things, too.

5. The fifth candle is for our adoptive parents ~ the parents we have now - the parents helping us to grow and who are learning to help us light our past so that we can understand.

6. The sixth candle is for the people who have helped us along the way, helping us to learn to like ourselves and to trust adults who can keep us safe.

7. The seventh candle is the best of all ~ it is for ourselves and our future. It is light for all of the wonderful things we are going to do in the future.

Allow adequate time for the child or youth to be still with their thoughts throughout the ceremony.

When using the ceremony with parents, adapt the meanings for each of the candles to match the unique circumstance of that parent.

Tips and techniques to making the activity meaningful:

When we experience a loss, whether it is the end of a relationship, the death of a loved one, or relocating to a new town leaving behind friends, family, and all that is familiar, we grieve. We all acknowledge that grieving is normal and healthy and expected. There are many rituals surrounding loss through death; participation in rituals can provide relief from the isolating feelings that accompany grief. For children and youth in foster care, there is often no ritual to recognize and validate the feelings of loss for people who have impacted their lives. Rituals can provide the permission that the child or youth needs to express his deepest thoughts and feelings about loved ones from whom he is separated. The act of lighting a candle in honor of those who have died is a centuries old tradition, and it can be adapted for use by children and youth in foster care. Workers can use the concept illustrated here, or modify elements of the ceremony to meet the individual needs of the child or youth. This is also an activity that could be considered in which groups of youth can participate.

Another way to help children and youth remember loved ones, particularly around the holidays, is to help the youth create a memory tree. A small artificial tree two to three feet high can be provided to the youth. Pictures of loved ones can then be placed in ornament frames (many craft stores carry these) and hung on the tree.

Notes/Adaptations:

Name of Activity: Collages

Key Concept: Working with Family Relationships and Loyalty

Primary Questions: Where Am I Going?   How Will I Get There?

Purpose: To create a visual representation of likes, dislikes, important people, places, events and memories into an art piece that represents the whole of the child/youth/family.

Materials Needed: Newspapers/magazines, ribbons, bits of colored or hand-made papers, portions of other artwork, copies of photographs, any other important objects that can be fastened to a canvas or poster board, glue, scissors, markers, crayons, pens/pencils.

Getting Started: Assemble materials and explain that the goal is to create a poster that represents something of meaning to the child/youth. You might suggest a collage of all the important people in their life or one that depicts important places. Give some ideas and direction, but remember to allow the child/youth/family to follow his/her own path. The collage might be a project that is developed over several meetings.

Tips and techniques to making the activity meaningful: Ask about the choices of materials and allow the individual to share if he likes. Remember not to get in the way by talking too much, follow the lead of the child/youth/family and validate feelings that may be expressed along the way.

Notes/Adaptations:

Name of Activity: Divide Your Life In Thirds

Key Concept: Working with Family Relationships and Loyalty

Primary Questions: Where Am I Going?   How Will I Get There?

Purpose: To provide a context for talking about the typical experiences of children/youth in care and to acknowledge the difficult and sometimes adult-like experiences that the child/youth may have endured. To recognize the resiliency of the child/youth and provide a sense of hope for the future.

Materials Needed: Sheet of paper and pen

Getting Started: Explain to the child/youth that he is going to be asked to think about his life in terms of three stages: childhood, teen and adult. Fold a sheet of paper into three columns, listing one of the three stages at the top of each column.

Ask the child/youth to think of some things that he has done, been through, or important events that occurred in each stage of his life. Challenge the child/youth to take a look at his childhood and teen years and see if the things that occurred are things that all children go through or has he experienced hardships that have made him stronger. For the adult stage, encourage the child/youth to list what he'd like to accomplish as an adult and what will it take to make that happen. You can also point out all of the things that he may have done in his life (taking care of siblings, cooking dinners, etc) that are really adult roles. Talk about how all of this has shaped him into the person they are today.

Tips and techniques to making the activity meaningful: Generally, most of our kids have had difficult pasts and they tend to list things that occur in the adult stages as things they did when they were children. Children/youth may fail to include events that occurred like their removal from birth home, which is often a life altering event. It's important to make note of this and challenge the child/youth to see his life in terms of what he has been through in his young years. Challenge the child/youth to take a look at his life events and decide what has made him stronger. Also, challenge him to see into his future and what he will need to do to accomplish his goals.

Notes/Adaptations:

Name of Activity: Dream a Little Dream

Key Concept: Working with Family Relationships and Loyalty

Primary Questions: Where Am I Going?   How Will I Get There?

Purpose: To address confusion the child/youth may feel related to the question Where Am I Going?

Materials Needed: Worksheet with a picture of a person sleeping with a "dream bubble" overhead, markers or crayons

Getting Started: Ask the child/youth to draw a picture of her dreams or wishes. Ask the child/youth to tell you about her picture. Initially this exercise can be used to get to know the child, but as time goes on, it can be repeated to help the child identify such things as what she envision when she is reunified with her family, what she wants in a new family or how she will know when she is accepted into her adoptive family. These later discussions will take more time and should present opportunities to address some of the confusion the child may feel about what a family is and what it means to belong to a family.

Tips and techniques to making the activity meaningful: Because drawing does not require a lot of conversation, it is often less threatening and provides an opportunity for the worker to engage the child/youth and create a safe environment.

Notes/Adaptations:

Name of Activity: Family Connections

Key Concept: Working with Family Relationships and Loyalty

Primary Questions: Where Am I Going?   How Will I Get There?

Purpose: To help children identify their support system and to help them realize they have connections they take with them throughout their lives. This exercise is also used to help the child in self-identity and to raise self-esteem.

Materials Needed: End roll of newsprint (can be obtained from local newspaper publisher), markers

Getting Started: Talk to the child/youth about the things he enjoys and the people he knows. Talk about the way he is different from some and how he shares common bonds with others. Roll out a sheet of newsprint larger than the child/youth. Ask the child/youth to lie on the newsprint and trace his outline. Talk about who he connects with in the following categories:

- Family (some will give the names of their birth families and foster families)
- Friends (can include past or present)
- School (can include teachers, guidance counselors, others)
- Church (members of congregation, pastor)
- Sports or After School Activities (coaches or instructors)

After each category, write the name of the person or activity by the part of the body the child associates with that person or activity. For example, names of family members may be placed by the heart, school connections near the child's head, sports related connections near hands and feet. After each section discuss how the child made these connections and their relative importance. This exercise is to be used to help the child define who he is and who his supports are. Reinforce these concepts throughout the activity.

Tips and techniques to making the activity meaningful: Depending on the age of the child and his ability to express himself, the people or activities identified by the child can be drawn instead of written. This activity should be used after a relationship has been established with the child.

Notes/Adaptations:

Name of Activity: Family Mobile

Key Concept: Working with Family Relationships and Loyalty

Primary Questions: Where Am I Going? How Will I Get There?

Purpose: To normalize for the child/youth that there can be confusion when people come into or move out of families until each person in the family is able to sort out his/her role.

Materials Needed: String, Scissors, paper plates, card stock, markers/crayons, paper clips, paper punch

Getting Started: Ask the child/youth to draw a picture of each member of her permanent family (birth, foster/adoptive, pre-adoptive, kinship) on a separate piece of card stock. Have her also draw a picture of herself. Punch one hole in the paper plate for each family member at even intervals (do not make a hole yet for the child/youth). Make sure there is a hole in the center of the paper plate in order to hang the mobile. Attach strings to each of the family members and attach them to the paper clips to hang in the holes on the paper plate. The mobile should be able to hang evenly.

Once this is complete, make another hole in the plate for the child/youth and hang her picture on the mobile. Discuss with the child/youth what happens to the mobile (it becomes   unbalanced). Discuss with the child/youth how moving into the family can cause unbalance in the family system as everyone is trying to figure out their new roles. The child/youth's adoptive parents are trying to figure out what the child likes/dislikes, how best to help the child and how to parent them. The child/youth is trying to figure out the family rules and what is expected of him in his new family (or in his birth family of child/youth is being reunified). The siblings are also trying to figure out how a new sibling fits into the family. Have another plate ready to punch new holes at equal intervals for everyone in the family, including the child. Move the family members to the new plate. Explain to the child as time goes on and everyone in the family adjusts to each other and figures out their new roles in the family (the child included) equilibrium returns to the family.

Tips and techniques to making the activity meaningful: If the child/youth has experiences placements that have been instable, encourage recalling of specific examples that contributed to an "unbalanced" system. Also discuss specific examples of times when the child/youth was part of a more "balanced" family system.

Notes/Adaptations:

Name of Activity: Family Ties

Key Concept: Working with Family Relationships and Loyalty

Primary Questions: Where Am I Going?   How Will I Get There?

Purpose: To help the child/youth honor family members, both past and present.

Materials Needed: Variety of beads, stringing material, paper and writing utensils

Getting Started: Ask the child to brainstorm characteristics of a family (i.e. people who take care of you, people who help you solve problems, people who give you physical traits such as hair and eye color). Engage in a discussion with the child/youth about members of their family, including foster family, birth family, and anyone else who the child views as being a member of his or her family. Ask the child/youth to make a list of all of these members. Then, for each person on the list, ask the child to choose a bead that represents each person. String the beads into a necklace, bracelet, or keychain. This finished product is something tangible the child/youth can keep close by as a reminder of the people he/she cares about and those who care about him/her.

Inevitably, discussion will arise about members of the child/youth's family. Be prepared to actively listen and perhaps journal some of the discussion for the child. Talk about how all of the members are different, as is represented by the different bead choices, but they are all linked together as members of that child/youth's family.

Tips and techniques to making the activity meaningful: Involve the child in going to the store with you to choose a variety of beads that they can later choose from when doing the exercise. Ask the child/youth selects beads each member, ask the child/youth to talk about why they chose each bead (these can be recorded for the Lifebook as well). Additional beads may be added as the child recalls more members or when an adoptive family is identified.

Notes/Adaptations:

Name of Activity: Loss Rocks

Key Concept: Working with Family Relationships and Loyalty

Primary Questions: Where Am I Going?   How Will I Get There?

Purpose: This activity helps to validate losses, and helps the child/youth begin to makes sense of the multiple losses he/she has experienced. This activity provides a healthy and effective way to express feelings of loss.

Materials Needed: Paper, pencil/pen, various sized rocks, an empty bag

Getting Started: Give the child/youth a blank piece of paper and a pencil and ask him to write down the different things he has lost in his life (i.e. contact/information about his siblings, time with birth parents, freedom/control of his life, a sibling who died, moving to many different homes). On the back of the paper, have him write down the hurts he has experienced (i.e. broken promises, birth parents not meeting their goals, being abused, people saying untruthful or hurtful things). Next talk about how each hurt or loss we experience is like a stone or rock being dropped in our heart. Some things that happen to us feel like a little pebble but other things feel like a big boulder. Get out the bag of various sized rocks that you brought along, showing him there are different sizes and shapes. Some are really ugly and dirty and jagged, others more clean and smooth. Give him an empty bag and direct his attention the list of losses and hurts. Starting at the top of the list, ask the child/youth to pick out a rock that represents the loss/hurt in his life and put it into his bag. For some of the things on the list, like broken promises, he may want to pick out several small and medium-sized rocks. After completing going through the list again, ask the child/youth to lift up the bag and see how heavy it feels. Relate that to how he might be feeling inside. Next, talk with him about carrying that load. Discuss with the child/youth how he has dealt with these things.

Tips and techniques to making the activity meaningful: Some children and youth may be ready to explore the concept of forgiveness. The worker can explain that holding on to the hurts can "weigh him down", possibly causing more anger, depression, and bitterness. Ask him if there were any of the rocks he feels like he could (or already has) let go of in his life. Have the child go through the pile and take away some of the rocks representing the hurts he has let go. If there are any remaining in the pile he has not let go, then talk about the things those rocks represented. Encourage the child to continue working at the grieving process for those remaining rocks so he can eventually remove all of them from the bag and experience the weight being lifted in his life. A discussion about coping strategies may be part of this activity (talking to people about the experiences/hurts, journaling, crying). Be prepared to be creative and actively listen to the child. Child's information can also be used in the child's Lifebook.

Notes/Adaptations:

Name of Activity: My Family Clay Icon

Key Concept: Working with Family Relationships and Loyalty

Primary Questions: Where Am I Going? How Will I Get There?

Purpose: This activity can be used to help both the child/youth and resource parent(s) understand that perceptions are important and changes happen.

Materials Needed: Clay or Play-Doh

Getting Started: Provide each participant with a lump of clay/container of Play-Doh (color is not necessarily important, unless it is to the child/youth). Instruct participants to create a simple sculpture that depicts some aspect of themselves (examples: someone who likes to garden may make a flower or plant, someone who likes to play video games may make a game controller, someone who is into music may make an instrument, CD, or music note). Also instruct the participants to not say what they will be sculpting or talk about it during the time they are working. Once all have completed their mini sculptures, have the participants exchange them (again, not discussing what they are). Each child should exchange with a resource parent/other family member. Then, with sculptures exchanged, instruct the participants to make changes (this is why no discussions should take place during construction; those sculptures not easily identified may not be understood).

After this phase is completed, ask the following questions of each participant regarding the participants' original sculptures:

- What was your sculpture and why did you make it?
- What were your thoughts when _____ changed it?
- What do you think of the changes that were made?
- Regarding changing the sculpture of another:
- What did you think the sculpture was?
- Why did you make the changes you did?

Depending on the level of connectivity among family members, this may be an easy activity, with no hurt feelings about the changes or it may incite a great deal of discussion. Point out to participants that how they perceive themselves may not be how others perceive them. Also point out how the modifications made were based on the viewer's interpretation and meant to depict the item more clearly or to help it fit in with the viewer's perception.

Tips and techniques to making the activity meaningful: This activity involves the child/youth and at least one resource parent. It can be done with sibling groups with all children participating at the same time. Birth children/other permanent members of the family may also participate—depending on the child/youth's level of comfort. Ideally, you have each child matched up with a resource parent/other permanent family member.

Notes/Adaptations:

Name of Activity: People I've Known

Key Concept: Working with Family Relationships and Loyalty

Primary Questions: Where Am I Going? How Will I Get There?

Purpose: To put together some missing pieces of the child's history, as well as give some closure to relationships that did not end well or did not have formal good-byes.

Materials Needed: Camera (video and/or photographs), child/youth's history (including names, address, phone numbers of important people), paper, markers, crayons, pens, glue/tape, stickers

Getting Started: Start by asking the child/youth to identify people who have been important in her life, (examples are, former foster parents, siblings, extended family, teachers, therapists, caseworkers, friends, CASA volunteers). Also, gather information from current people whom the child/youth is close to, and from case records. Then, contact these people to ask if they would be willing to contribute to the child/youth's Lifebook. This can be done by letter for former foster parents and people who knew the child in her early history. Phone calls work best for people whom are likely to remember the child easily. Each individual's contribution can be decided by that person, but suggestions to offer include, a letter to the child, meeting the child in person, photographs, and/or time spent reminiscing. If you do not get a response from the people you have contacted, you can simply talk to the child about these individuals, reminding him/her about their time together, and asking the child to tell you what she remembers about each person. While not as effective, it can still be helpful for the child to recall those who have been significant in her life.

Lifebook pages can be created by the child for each person, stating their name, where and when they knew him, and any memories that they have of that person, and the time the child spent with them.

Tips and techniques to making the activity meaningful: It can be helpful to begin with the child/youth's most recent history, as this may be the least anxiety producing. Some children/youth may not be able to recall many of the people who have been in their lives, but will remember them when they see or hear from them again. It can be comforting for children/youth to discover that others remember them and have thought of them since they have moved on. The worker can also talk with the child/youth about the things he learned from each person, or the impact that the person had on his life. This may need to be prompted more for younger children, or children with limited insight.

Notes/Adaptations:

Name of Activity: People Remembered Chart

Key Concept: Working with Family Relationships and Loyalty

Primary Questions: Where Am I Going?   How Will I Get There?

Purpose: To help recognize that there are many people in their lives who love and care about them.

Materials Needed: Pens, markers, crayons, camera/pictures, paper

Getting Started: Begin by talking about the idea that each of us have people in our lives who love and care about us. Have the individual brainstorm a list of people in her life who loves and cares about her (the child/youth/family may need your help, give suggestions if needed). Help construct a chart that allows a column for each person's name, relationship, and ways that person shows that they care. Have the individual consider ways each person shows that they care, and record the answers on the chart. Encourage the inclusion of caregivers as well as others, such as friends, to their list.

Tips and techniques to making the activity meaningful: This activity presents a very good opportunity to remember and honor those that have been lost through separation, including birth parents, siblings, aunts/uncles, friends, and teachers to name a few. Use the activity to prompt stories and memories related to each individual identified. *Listen and be present* as the child/youth/family expresses his/her feelings related to each important person.

Notes/Adaptations:

Name of Activity: Sands of Time and Place

Key Concept: Working with Family Relationships and Loyalty

Primary Questions: Where Am I Going?   How Will I Get There?

Purpose: To help the child/youth see how the past and the future are connected.

Materials Needed: Different colors of sand, a small container, a teaspoon

Getting Started: After identifying the number of placements, (including birth, foster, residential, and adoptive), ask the child/youth to identify a color of sand for each of the different places he lived. Then, using the teaspoon, place one teaspoon of sand in the jar for each year (time can also be captured in terms of months) of the child's life in each place, using the colors to match the placements as identified by the child.

Tips and techniques to making the activity meaningful: The colored sand will form layers in the jar, allowing the child/youth to see their various placements in relation to each other. Talk with the child about the importance of each placement, recognizing the significance of all the placements by asking the child for his thoughts about each of them. The worker can suggest ideas such as how important the past is; if the child lived with his birth family most of his life and is wishing he were still there, point out how much more sand there is related to this time, compared to the rest. If instead the child wants to "forget" a placement, demonstrate that all of the colors blend together to make us who we are, and that in time, the sand that corresponds to that place will seem like less than it does now.   It is likely that the child will stir the sand in the jar so that it is all mixed together. This is actually a good demonstration of integration, and can again be used to show the child how much and how little sand there is related to each placement. (In the example above, the sand of the birth family will be the most prevalent, even when all of the grains of sand are mixed together.)

Notes/Adaptations:

Name of Activity: Sibling Placements

Key Concept: Working with Family Relationships and Loyalty

Primary Questions: Where Am I Going?   How Will I Get There?

Purpose: Honors the past, and the child/youth's journey and out-of-home placements with and without siblings. Also validates feelings associated with being placed together and/or separately.

Materials Needed: : 8.5 x 11 card stock cut outs of houses, each labeled with the name and address of each home the children have lived in (preferably with a picture of each family, whether birth or foster).

Getting Started: Lay each house cut-out on the floor in a Lifemap pattern. The Lifemap should follow each child's placement. If a sibling was separated from the others in a different home, place that home next to the sibling's home. Explain to the children that they started out in their birth parents home (or wherever their first placement was) and show how they moved from one home to the next with their siblings. If there was a separation, ask the separated child to step to their separate home. When reunited, ask all the children to step back together on the home where they were reunited. With each step to another home, discuss how it felt to move to another home. Discuss memories of that foster home/family. Discuss how each child felt about being placed together/separate/reunited. Explain to the siblings that even though they did not live together in every home, they are still a family. Stress the importance of being together.

Tips and techniques to making the activity meaningful: This activity can be completed once the worker has met with the children several times and has established a relationship with all of the siblings.

Notes/Adaptations:

Name of Activity: String Exercise

Key Concept: Working with Family Relationships and Loyalty

Primary Questions: Where Am I Going? How Will I Get There?

Purpose: To help the child/youth determine who is in his life, his level of support and/or attachment to each individual, and who he would like to continue contact with if he moves to a new family.

Materials Needed: String or yarn, scissors, tape, index cards, markers

Getting Started: Discuss with the child/youth the different individuals in his life who are important to him (friends, foster family, former caregivers, birth family members, therapists, teachers, social workers). Ask the child/youth to write each individual's name on a separate index card, making sure he includes one index card with his name on it. Tape the index card with the child/youth's name on a wall or place it on the floor making sure you have lots of room around the card. Next begin talking about each individual written on the other cards, highlighting how strong of an attachment the child/youth has with that individual. Attach a string from the child's card to each individual's card to denote the bond between the child and the individual. The shorter the string between the child/youth and the individual on the card, the closer or stronger the bond; the longer the string, the more distant the bond. If the child no longer has contact with any of the individuals on the index cards, then cut the string close to the child's card (leaving a small end hanging). If the child is moving, discuss with the child who he wants to continue contact with after he moves, as well as those they may not have contact with, such as teachers, therapists, and so on. Cut the strings for any individual who will not or may not have contact with the child after he/she moves. Each cut string represents a loss the child has experienced in their lives.

Tips and techniques to making the activity meaningful: Discussion topics from this activity may include, but are not limited to support the child/youth does/does not receive from each individual, plans regarding who the child/youth would like to maintain contact with, separation and loss if the relationship is not as close as the child/youth desires, feelings of hurt surrounding birth family members or former caregivers.

Notes/Adaptations:

Name of Activity: Water Pitcher Exercise

Key Concept: Working with Family Relationships and Loyalty

Primary Questions: Where Am I Going?   How Will I Get There?

Purpose: To provide a visual representation of all of the families who have been important to the child/youth and to demonstrate how experiences with each contribute to whom the child/youth is today. To help children understand they do not have to give up people in the past to love new people.

Materials Needed: Large (at least ½ gallon) pitcher, assortment of different sized glasses

Getting Started: Explain to the child that the pitcher represents him and, like all kids, he was born empty. (Look inside the pitcher, shake it, etc.) Explain that when we are babies we need so much – to be fed, played with, loved, and changed. Explain that when the child was born his birth mom took them home and did the best she could. (Pick up a glass size - depends on how long the child lived there.) Fill up the glass. "Your mom gave you your eyes, hair, etc., but she couldn't give you all you needed" (empty water into the pitcher). (Show the child how much more room is in the pitcher.) "Do you know why?" (Talk about the reason, alcohol/mental illness, etc.) "So you went to your first foster home and were only there a short time (use smaller glass) so they gave you all they could (fill glass) can they give you more?", " No." Add to the pitcher. "Now look -- part is your birth mom and part is your foster mom. Which part is which?" (Child is puzzled.) "Right, they are both inside of you and part of you always. You don't give up one, just add." Do a glass for each foster home. Use the appropriate size of glass depending on length of time in home. Do not make value judgments as to quality of care, just address the time in each home. (Make sure you don't fill the pitcher). Then say "the people who want to adopt you want to fill you up." (Take the pitcher to the sink and run the water slowly in it.) "They want to give you what you need to be a good adult. They want to add to your past, not take it away. You keep your past with you and love those people always." Wait for the pitcher to overflow. "Adoption means a family who can fill you up and have enough love and caring left for your children, their grandchildren."

Tips and techniques to making the activity meaningful: Encourage the child to talk about each family as they fill the cups and to share stories that are meaningful to him or her about each. Remember that difficult or challenging experiences also help make us who we are, so don't be tempted to have the child talk only about positive experiences; talking about painful experiences is part of the healing process. For children who are being reunified with their families, omit reference to adoptive families and instead add more water to the pitcher representing the child's family who will continue to nurture them into adulthood.

Credit: Regina M. Kupecky, MAT, LSW

Notes/Adaptations:

Name of Activity: Writing Letters

Key Concept: Working with Family Relationships and Loyalty

Primary Questions: Where Am I Going?   How Will I Get There?

Purpose: To provide a safe way for the expression of feelings toward someone who has hurt the child/youth or from who the child/youth as been separated. Writing is a very therapeutic activity, especially for those who are less outwardly expressive. Many children/youth find they can vent a great deal of grief and frustration by 'putting it to pen and paper' when they are not able to express it in any other way. He can begin to process his fears, concerns, excitement, and other feelings through the written word.

Materials Needed: Paper, pens and pencils, envelopes

Getting Started: Invite the child/youth to sit down and write a letter to anyone he feels he would like to address (birth parents, caseworkers, foster parents, prospective adoptive parents, siblings, therapists, teachers). If the child is hesitant to write, you can assist him in actually writing the letter as he instructs you regarding what he would like to say. A suggested outline for the letter includes the following elements:

- What happened that caused the hurt or separation?
- What haven't you said that you might now be ready to say?
- What are your feelings about it?
- What do you now like about what happened?
- What are some good things about what happened?
- What would you like to see happen next?

Tell the child that he does not have to send the letter, but he can use it as a way to say some of the things he would like to convey to the person he is writing to. Once the letter is composed, have the child place it in a sealed envelope and help him to decide what should happen with the letter next. Children who are unable to write can put their ideas to paper in the form of a picture story and seal it up in an envelope just as you would do with a letter.

Tips and techniques to making the activity meaningful: Sometimes it will be appropriate to mail this letter, other times it will not. Help the child/youth to determine how he should use the letter, keeping in mind that the goal is for this activity to be beneficial to the child in some way, not to be vengeful or vindictive to another person who may have hurt him. In addition to writing to people the child/youth already knows, this can also be a great activity for helping a child address his "ideal family" and let them know his expectations, before a family is even identified.

Notes/Adaptations:

Transfer of Learning

Consider the following questions to enhance your understanding of the task of Integration:

Think about a time that you experienced traumatic event or suffered the loss of a loved one. How did this event impact you at that time? What influence does the event have on who you are today?

What do you believe is the most important life lesson you have ever learned? How did you learn this valuable lesson?

Who are the most important persons in your life? How do they influence your feelings about your experiences? How do you resolve feelings of hurt, anger, confusions from persons whom you feel close to?

Activities Related to Actualization

Name of Activity: All in the Family

Key Concept: Working with Belonging to Families

Primary Questions: When Will I Know I Belong?

Purpose: To explore significant people in the child/youth/family's life; those who the individual defines as "family".

Materials Needed: Paper, markers, crayons, pens or pencils

Getting Started: Ask child/youth/family to draw a picture of her family. Assure her that there are no wrong answers and encourage the individual to draw family as she defines it. Have the individual label each family member in the drawing. Remember to allow the individual to direct this activity. Encourage discussion, but try not to make the individual feel as though she should or should not include certain individuals.

Tips and techniques to making the activity meaningful: If the drawing does not include obvious family members (parents, siblings, etc) raise this for discussion. Similarly, if the drawing includes non-traditional family members such as caseworkers or favorite teachers, talk about this as well, again in the context of the meaning the child/youth/family defines.

Notes/Adaptations:

Name of Activity: Celebration Countdown Chain

Key Concept: Working with Belonging to Families

Primary Questions: When Will I Know I Belong?

Purpose: To provide preparation for occasions such as an adoption hearing, placement with a new family, reunification with the family, holiday, birthday or family event. This activity promotes family interaction and helps children to recognize how important they are to the family.

Materials Needed: Colored construction paper, marker, tape, and scissors

Getting Started: Cut strips of construction paper. This can either be done ahead of time or with the child. Write down positive statements on each strip of paper. The statements should include positive things about each family member, how each member is important to the family, special family memories, traditions, and things that make the family special and unique. Make one strip for each day as they countdown to the special event. For example, if the adoption hearing is 30 days away, the chain should include 30 strips of paper, each with a statement on it. Connect the paper strips together to form a chain.

Tips and techniques to making the activity meaningful:

As the child/family counts down to the special event, a link of the chain is discussed once a day when all family members are present. The child or youth will be able to count the links remaining on the chain to know how many days until the special event.

Notes/Adaptations:

Name of Activity: Chain Link

Key Concept: Working with Belonging to Families

Primary Questions: When Will I Know I Belong?

Purpose: To demonstrate the ways that family members are connected to one another, despite their similarities or differences.

Materials Needed: Strips of colorful construction paper cut into 1" x 6" strips, glue, markers, crayons, pens, pencils

Getting Started: Suggest that being part of a family is like the links of a chain, each is individual and yet, connected to all others on the chain. Have the child/youth/family identify each member of a family and decorate a link for each family member. Have them put the links together to represent the family. As they are doing this, talk about who each member is and what meaning they have. This allows the expression of both positive and negative feelings for those they have experienced as a family member.

Tips and techniques to making the activity meaningful: Remember that the individual can put whomever he/she wants on their chain. He may chose to keep adding people or removing people as he works over time on family membership. This activity helps to increase awareness of family qualities that are valued, assuring his/her needs for ongoing or future permanent relationships.

Notes/Adaptations:

Name of Activity: Dream Catcher

Key Concept: Working with Belonging to Families

Primary Questions: When Will I Know I Belong?

Purpose: To provide a visual representation of the relationships and other connections in the individual's life and to provide an opportunity to explore the permanence of their relationships.

Materials Needed: Paper plate, yarn, hole punch, craft beads and feathers, markers, scissors

Getting Started: Cut the center out of the plate, leaving about 2 inches around the diameter. Punch holes around the rim of the paper plate, about ½ inch apart. Measure a piece of yarn about 5-6 feet long. Tie one end of the yarn to one of the holes on the rim of the paper plate, and then weave the yarn through the other holes, in any pattern, using all of the holes. Beads, feathers and other strands of yarn can be added to the Dream Catcher as the individual chooses. After all of the holes are threaded with the yarn, tie a knot at the end. Punch three additional holes at the bottom of the plate and cut three more pieces of yarn, about 5 inches long each. Take each piece of yarn and tie them to the three holes at the bottom of the Dream Catcher. Thread beads onto each of the three yarn pieces and then tie a feather to the end each. Decorate the edges of the paper plate with markers. To hang punch one last hole at the top of the page and fasten another piece of yarn to the hole for hanging.

Tips and techniques to making the activity meaningful: Suggest that a Dream Catcher can "catch" items, and for the purpose of this activity, a Dream Catcher represents people who have been important to the child/youth. Use this as an opportunity to talk about relationships in terms of permanency, suggesting that some relationships are more permanent than others. Encourage the child/youth/family to talk about some of the relationships in their lives, comparing and contrasting those that are more permanent than others. Explore the importance of past relationships, noting that often relationships are meaningful to an individual despite the distance of time or space. Allowing the child/youth to select the yarn, beads, and feathers used for the activity can make it more meaningful.

Notes/Adaptations:

Name of Activity: Family Collages

Key Concept: Working with Belonging to Families

Primary Questions: When Will I Know I Belong?

Purpose: To help the child/youth consider what family is and begin to see him or herself as part of a family.

Materials Needed: Magazines, scissors, glue, paper, markers, stickers

Getting Started: Give the child/youth several magazines to look through. Ask the child/youth to cut out pictures of families. These can include parents, siblings, pets, or whatever the child/youth defines as a picture representing a family. After several pictures have been cut out, ask the child/youth to sort the pictures into categories that describe what families are or what families do. Some example categories include: families have fun together; families provide food and shelter, families care about each other. Have the child then make a collage of each group of pictures and give it a title, such as "belonging", "safety", and "caring" as these words relate to the previous example categories.

Tips and techniques to making the activity meaningful: As you and the child/youth work on cutting, sorting and gluing, talk about the concept of family and what "real" families are like. Point out that all families have rules and chores and all families argue at times. Talk about how families define who belongs and what makes the family members feel like they belong. Children can draw pictures or add stickers to their collages. Younger children may need help sorting and giving a name to the categories.

Notes/Adaptations:

Name of Activity: Family Home-Future Home

Key Concept: Working with Belonging to Families

Primary Questions: When Will I Know I Belong?

Purpose: To begin to address a transition from reunification to adoption.

Materials Needed: White paper, colored pencils, crayons, and/or markers

Getting Started: Ask the child/youth to create a picture of his birth home. Ask child to draw a picture of the home he lived in with their birth family. Ask him to describe it as he draws it. Ask him to share things that happened in different rooms in the house. Encourage the sharing of positive and negative things. What was his favorite room and why? What was his least favorite room and why? What were the feelings he had when they lived in that house?

Then ask the child/youth to draw a picture of his "future" home. Ask him to describe it as he draws it. Ask him who will live in the house with him. How will this house be different than the house he lived in with his birth family?

How will this house feel different than his birth family home?

Tips and techniques to making the activity meaningful: In relationship to the picture of his birth home, encourage the child to identify positive and negative things about her birth family. If possible, try to encourage a balanced view of her birth family, honoring both positive and negative elements. In relationship to the "future" home, ask the child/youth to identify those things that will be the same and different in her future home than they were in the birth family home. If the focus is on material things try to encourage the inclusion of emotional aspects by asking things like "How it will feel in this home and what type of interactions will occur between the members of the household?" Talk about what he can do to make these differences come about.

Notes/Adaptations:

Name of Activity: Fitting In

Key Concept: Working with Belonging to Families

Primary Questions: When Will I Know I Belong?

Purpose: To talk about transitions and how things sometimes change.

Materials Needed: Worksheet titled "I'll Know I Fit In When..." that has the following questions listed on it with space to record answers below each: The family..., The kids at school..., The relatives..., The neighbors treat me like..., The members of my birth family say...

Getting Started: Talk to the child/youth about what "fitting in" means. Ask him about other places he has been and how long it took for him to feel comfortable. Ask what was happening when he felt comfortable. For children/youth who have never been comfortable, this is a dream page. After the discussion, take out the worksheet. Have the child/youth fill in under each category the ways he will know when he fits in.

Tips and techniques to making the activity meaningful: Be prepared with lots of examples to get the child/youth thinking.

Notes/Adaptations:

Name of Activity: How Well Do You Know Your Family?

Key Concept: Working with Belonging to Families

Primary Questions: When Will I Know I Belong?

Purpose: To help the family members get to know the child/youth better (and vice versa), as in a new placement, or after a child has been in a family for a longer period of time and is beginning to feel he or she belongs. This can even be done between siblings, whether they live together or are just visiting with each other. This can also be used as part of family visitation and reunification.

Materials Needed: Several copies of the questions below, small prizes (optional)

Getting Started: Each person writes the answers to the questions first (without letting others see the answers). Then one person guesses the answers for the other person and vice versa. Give small prizes for correct answers (pennies, small candy pieces, marbles).

Encourage the family members to discuss the answers and make it fun. The point of this activity is to help family members learn about each other in a fun way. From their answers, point out similarities and differences between members in their likes, habits, and experiences.

For the younger children or those who have difficulty reading the questions or writing the answers, the worker can read or write for them. Hints can be given when the child/youth tries to guess the answers of the adults and questions can be deleted or added depending on the situation, age, and ability of the child.

1. Where were you born (city or town)?
2. What is your favorite food?
3. What is your favorite color?
4. What is your favorite TV show?
5. What is your favorite movie?
6. How many states have you lived in?
7. Who is your best friend?
8. Would you rather go on vacation to the beach, the mountains, or the city?
9. What is your favorite sport?
10. What is your favorite sports team?
11. What kind of music do you like?
12. What is your favorite animal?
13. What is your best skill or trait?
14. Are you a morning or an evening person (do you like to get up early or stay up late)?
15. What is your favorite book?
16. What is (was) your favorite subject in school?
17. What is your favorite season of the year (spring, summer, fall, winter)?
18. What is your favorite holiday?
19. If you could have any job in the world, what would it be?
20. What is your biggest dream for the future?

Tips and techniques to making the activity meaningful: This activity can be played as a game between any family members (two at a time), whether biological, foster, or adoptive; siblings or parents. Many children and youth enjoy this game. It provides a non-threatening way to share information about them, but also to learn more about others.

Notes/Adaptations:

Name of Activity: Thanks for Being Part of Me

Key Concept: Working with Belonging to Families

Primary Questions: When Will I Know I Belong?

Purpose: To highlight the unique qualities that the child/youth brings to her family (whether birth of adoptive). To provide an opportunity for the child to talk about each family member and for each member to reciprocate.

Materials Needed: Paper, markers, crayons, pens, camera

Getting Started: Start by taking a picture of the child with each member of her family. Then have each family member state why they are glad this child is a member of their family. This could be anything from positive personality characteristics to favorite shared activities. Each person should then illustrate this by making a page with a picture, and/or words, such as "My favorite thing about Alex is..." or "I'm glad that Jenny is my sister because..." Adults can help children write. To complete this activity, mount the corresponding photograph at the top of each family member's page. If the child is old enough, you can also have her make a page about what she likes best about each family member.

Tips and techniques to making the activity meaningful: This activity will help the child/youth and his or her family (especially siblings), talk about what it means to be a family. It can help to answer "Who am I?" by focusing on the unique traits that the child brings to the family. In addition, discussion can focus around the variety of families, and how each person contributes something unique to make the family a whole. It should help the child to feel more a part of the family unit, and should help to strengthen the familial bonds. In this way, it can help to answer the question "How will I know I Belong?"

This activity can be adapted for younger or non-communicative children by having caregivers contribute the child's point of view. For example, the page could have a picture of an infant with his older sister stating, "I like Mary because she reads me a story every night before I go to bed."

Notes/Adaptations:

Name of Activity: What You Need to Know About Me

Key Concept: Working with Belonging to Families

Primary Questions: When Will I Know I Belong?

Purpose: To help ease the anxieties of transitioning from one placement setting to another. Writing down how the child/youth acts when sad, what she does when angry, and what comforts her, may help her feel more at ease that future caretakers will have a better understanding of her and her feelings.

Materials Needed: Worksheet with the following questions and space to write under each:

- Sometimes I get angry and here is what I do to show my angry feelings
- Sometimes I get sad, usually when I think about….
- My feelings hurt when…and this is what I do….
- I get frustrated when…and this is what I do….
- Here is what scares me….
- …and when I am scared I act like this….
- The one thing I need to have with me to make me feel safe and secure is….
- This is what I do when I go to bed at night….
- The best time of day for me is….

Getting Started: Talk about the different ways kids act when faced with certain new situations. Some kids act wild when they are angry, others just sit and fume about the situation. Others need space to cool off, others will punch their pillow. Lead the conversation to talk about how scary it is to think about moving and how new caretakers may react to the child/youth expressing his feelings.

Explain to child/youth that you would like to talk about the next step for them. Examples could be moving from a foster home into a residential treatment center, from one relative to another, or from one foster home to another foster home. Express to the child/youth that this will give the people who will be caring for him a better idea of what the he is all about, how he reacts in certain situations, how he deals with feelings, and what he needs to be well cared for.

Tips and techniques to making the activity meaningful: Talking about ways kids deal with their emotions is always beneficial, at whatever stage they are in. By talking about how the child deals with difficult situations and what he does when he is sad, he may feel more at ease about his transition and more comfortable knowing that his new caretakers have been prepared for his arrival.

Pictures can be very helpful for children and youth who are being placed in out-of-home care or transitioning to a new placement setting. Providing a photo of the house, foster family, or residential staff in the next setting can provide the child with a sense of comfort when they arrive at the new setting. The child/youth can also be asked about favorite foods and the new caretakers can be asked to prepare some of these comfort foods in the first few days of the placement.

Notes/Adaptations:

Name of Activity: Yellow Brick Road

Key Concept: Working with Belonging to Families

Primary Questions: When Will I Know I Belong?

Purpose: To help the child/youth explore the type of family she would like to belong to. When an adoptive family is identified, the child may want to draw a picture of that family.

Materials Needed: Paper, markers, pens, pencils

Getting Started: Begin a discussion with the child/youth about the type of family she sees herself being a part of. Ask her to create on paper a picture of the type of family she would like to belong to on a permanent basis. Encourage her to be specific, for example, pets, race of family, who the members of the family might be. If the child is unsure about what she thinks her future family should look like, encourage her to draw several different pictures- the drawings can also include written words such as adjectives that the child may use to describe a potential adoptive family, for example: loving, caring, funny, active.

Tips and techniques to making the activity meaningful: This activity is best used when the child/youth is beginning to see themselves as members of another family. This is also a good point to help the child/youth appreciate the hard work she has done to get to the point of actualization.

Notes/Adaptations:

Transfer of Learning

Consider the following questions to enhance your understanding of the task of Actualization:

What long term goals have you identified for yourself? Have you thought about the steps to achieving it? Can you visualize yourself getting there? What skills have you/will you draw upon to achieve your goal? How will you know you are there?

Have you ever found yourself wondering about your path? Think about the feeling you had. If there was uncertainty, what did that feel like? Did you overcome this feeling? If so, how?

How do you know when you want to have a life long relationship with another? How do you assure ongoing relationships with the people that you love?

Engaging Children and Youth in Their Work

The following are some descriptions of the work that has been done and a reflection how the 3-5-7 Model was used:

A youth preparing to leave his foster family and move to his adoptive family talked about his recent vacation with his foster family to the beach. He was excited to explain how he had gone fishing and surfing in the ocean. In this example the child is working through the idea of separation from his foster family. He is visualizing himself transitioning to a new family—in essence actualizing this transition.

A youth who is aware of the reasons for her placement in foster care began her Life Book by decorating people she had drawn. She colored different people and named who they were and why they were colored different colors. She colored her birth mother and birth father's faces black. She shared that she did so because they were bad people. She went on to share that her father drinks a lot and gets very mean. She shared that she really misses her mother despite knowing that she is "bad." This is an example of a clarification activity. Children give meaning to the things that they create as they explore and express feelings. Our role is to listen and be present to that. It is not necessary for the worker to further interpret this with the child. It is also important to note that expressions of feelings are not absolute; they are often evolving. In other words, the child's perception may change over time, as she continues to explore and express her feelings.

A youth shared that her mother was incarcerated and that she would return home once her mother "got out of jail". The youth gave voice to her perception that her mother had done some bad things such as stealing. The worker introduced a book about how alcohol and drugs affect families. The youth was willing to read only a few pages of the book and then decided to move on. The youth in this example appears to be grieving for her mother and the life she had before foster care. This example of a clarification activity highlights the fact that children's expressions of grief are often short. Although children do not sustain expressions of grief for very long periods of time, that should not lead workers to believe that there is resolution of their grief. When the child feels safe with the person who participates in the activity with them, they will revisit their grief work.

To help the child integrate all his connections, beads were offered to create a piece of jewelry. Each bead was to represent significant people in the child's life. The child needed some help getting started, but after glancing at his Life Book a few times, he caught onto the idea. He created a very long line of beads; it surprised him how many people he was able to name. For some people, he took some time to find the right bead to represent the person he named. He placed a bead for his birth mother and foster mother next to one another. And he clustered birth family members together, foster family members together, and other outside influential people together. The activity concluded with the child sharing a special memory for each person he named. This integration activity illustrates that given the opportunity, children and youth can process and give meaning to the people in their lives. A simple introduction to the idea was all that was needed to support the work of the child in this session. The child gave the meaning that he wanted to each of the beads and their placement while the worker simply listened and was present to that expression. The result of the activity was a tangible symbol for the child.

The worker introduced an activity to a youth that involved answering questions about his likes and dislikes. He began to cry saying, "Don't waste my time, I will never be adopted", and "Why can't I just stay here?".

This example shows the importance of following the youth's lead in the process. The expression of his feelings of anxiety about separating from his foster family and fears that he might never truly belong in a family must be recognized and validated. Brief responses from the worker such as, "I know you are scared" or "The thought of leaving people that you care about is painful" might be most helpful in supporting the work of the youth in that moment.

The Significance of Photographs

Pictures are the visual stories of our lives. They evoke memories of past events, the important experiences and significant times of our life activities and the people who have participated with us in these moments. Each picture captures a moment in time that is frozen in memory. For children and youth who have lived with trauma in their lives, these pictures can provide reference points, both pleasing and or painful. Using pictures in life book work provides opportunities for children, youth, and families to explore their feelings related to the persons and/or events captured in the pictures. They are able to give meaning to the relationships. They are provided with a developmental view of where and who they have been. The visual representation affirms their existence and identity.

Each task of the 3-5-7 Model, clarification, integration and actualization is furthered by the use of pictures. Life events are clarified through the stories contained within the pictures; overall identity and information about previous families are integrated through pictures. No matter where they have been or where they are going, children and youth will have a visual validation of their lives. It lessens anxieties of the fears of not remembering important past family relationships, supports resolution of these lost relationships, and allows for moving forward.

The Use of Books and Movies to Support the Work

Many of us can relate to the circumstances of others, whether real or fictional, when we share an experience depicted in a movie or book. When we are engaged in the story of another, we are often exploring our own feelings related to that event in our own lives. For workers, movies can provide valuable insight into the feelings that may be experienced by the children, youth, and families with whom they work. Reading with children/youth books with themes that related to the child/youth's experiences can be validating and provide hope and healing opportunities.

Suggested Books:

A Mother for Choco by Keiko Kasza
Choco was a little bird who lived all alone. He wished he had a mother, but who could his mother be?

Adoption Stories for Young Children by Randall B. Hicks
This book shows real photos of real babies, kids, birthparents and adoptive parents. It explains in very simple terms why some parents cannot care for their children, and why they choose to make an adoption plan.

All Kinds of Families by Norma Simon
Explores in words and pictures what a family is and how families vary in makeup and styles.

Benjamin Bear Gets a New Family by Deborah Berry Joy
This book deals, in story-book form, with the feelings many children experience as a result of their birth parents inability to provide care for them, as well as feelings related to their subsequent adoption.

I Miss My Foster Parents by Stefon Herbert
This is a very simple book, written and illustrated by a child. The author was a foster child who was missed his foster parents after joining an adoptive family.

Finding the Right Spot: When Kids Can't Live with Their Parents by Janice Levy
Written for children who are living with anyone other than their parents, this story is narrated by a spirited young girl who is living with Aunt Dane (not her real aunt) for a while, until her mother is able to care for her again.

The Great Gilly Hopkins by Katherine Patterson
This is a story of eleven-year-old Gilly who has lived in multiple foster families and disliked them all. Gilly has a plan to get her "real mother" to come rescue her. The rescue doesn't work out, and Gilly is left thinking that maybe life with her foster parents isn't all that bad.

How it Feels to be Adopted by Jill Kremntz
Nineteen boys and girls, from age 8 - 16 and from every social background, confide their feelings about this crucial fact.

Is that Your Sister? by Catherine and Sherry Bunin
An adopted six-year-old girl tells about adoption and how she and her adopted sister feel about it.

Lucy's Feet by Stephanie Stein
Eight-year-old Lucy is suddenly uncomfortable with the meaning of being adopted by her parents, while her new baby brother was born to them.

Maybe Days: A Book for Children in Foster Care by Jennifer Wilgocki
Will I live with my parents again? Will I stay with my foster parents forever? For children in foster care, the answer to many questions is often "maybe." Maybe Days addresses the questions, feelings, and concerns these children most often face.

Pugnose Has Two Special Families by Karis Kruzel
Pugnose is a sweet little mouse who tells us his open adoption story. Pugnose tells us how he has a handsome nose like his birthfather and big ears like his birthmother and how happy he is to be part of two special families. This is the perfect book for children who are in an open adoption.

The Lost Boy: A Foster Child's Search for the Love of a Family by Dave J. Pelzer
This is Dave Pelzer's sequel to A Child Called "It". In The Lost Boy, he answers questions and reveals new adventures through the compelling story of his life as an adolescent. Now considered an F-Child (Foster Child), Dave is moved in and out of five different homes. He suffers shame and experiences resentment from those who feel that all foster kids are trouble and unworthy of being loved just because they are not part of a "real" family.

Three Little Words: A Memoir by Ashley Rhodes-Courter
Ashley Rhodes-Courter spent nine years of her life in fourteen different foster homes. As her mother spirals out of control, Ashley is left clinging to an unpredictable, dissolving relationship, all the while getting pulled deeper and deeper into the foster care system.

What's A Foster Family, Anyway? by Martine Golden Inlay
This easy-to-read book can assist children in the foster care system to understand terminology that is often confusing to them. There are pages for individual reflection at the end of the book.

Will You Take Care of Me? by Margaret Park Bridges
A warm, imaginative story that gently reminds young ones of a parent's unwavering devotion. No matter how her child grows or changes, Mama will always be there.

Zachary's New Home: A Story for Foster and Adopted Children by Geraldine M. and Paul Blomquist
This story for adopted and foster children describes the adventures of Zachary the kitten, who is taken from his mother's house when his mother is unable to take care of him. The book follows Zachary as he first goes into foster care and then is adopted by a family of geese.

Suggested Movies:

The Color Purple (1985)
Two sisters are separated from one another, the trauma of the physical separation is depicted.

Men Don't Leave (1990)
Expression of the grief of a 7 year old boy who lost his father.

Losing Isaiah (1995)
Overwhelming fear and ultimate exhaustion of a young boy as he is separated from his parent.

The Horse Whisperer (1998)
A scene in this movie about a horse healer who works with a girl who was hit by a truck when riding her horse shows how the whisperer waits patiently for the horse to be ready on its own terms.

A.I. Artificial Intelligence (2001)
A robotic boy longs to become "real" to be worthy of the love of his adoptive mother.

White Oleander (2002)
Teenager moves through several foster homes after her mother is incarcerated.

Rabbit Proof Fence (2002)
Story about the connection of three sisters who travel a long journey to be home with family.

The Blind Side (2009)
True story of Michael Oher, a homeless and traumatized boy is taken in by a family.

Dealing with Common Barriers

There are some common barriers that can discourage both the child/youth and workers from applying the 3-5-7 Model© concepts to their work. Here are some common barriers and some quick tips to address them.

Child/youth/family displays unwillingness to talk; seems disinterested:

- Let them know what to expect by telling them how long the session will last
- Explain your goals; that you are meeting with them to help them understand what has happened and to answer their questions
- Reassure them of the confidentiality
- Start with a relaxing activity, perhaps drawing your own life map
- Acknowledge that they may be feeling confused, sad, angry, etc.
- Use eye contact; however, do not expect them to maintain eye contact
- Work in short sessions
- Vary activities/tasks
- Don't become intimidated by their reluctance

Child/youth has difficulty writing:

- Write for the child/youth as you go along
- Assure the child that grammar isn't important
- Use a digital recorder or video camera to record the session
- Have the child/youth draw pictures to tell the story

Child is unfamiliar with materials:

- Show some simple examples
- Give the child assurance and encouragement

Worker feels inexperienced or unsure:

- Look at other Lifebooks
- Remember that the child/family's input is what is most important
- Practice
- Assure yourself that the Lifebook is for the child/youth
- Remember that children and youth y can benefit from the chance to face many unresolved emotions
- Remember that over time, the Lifebook should be a stabilizing force and give a sense of identity

In general terms, be familiar with many different activities and always have with you materials such as stickers, paper, markers/crayons, beads, glue, scissors, actual pictures of child/youth/family life or magazines, and other various materials that child or youth can engage with. Keep the materials within view of the child/youth/family.

While these ideas may be useful in overcoming the circumstances that may get in the way of a worker supporting the child/youth in clarification, integration and actualization, one of the most important ways that a worker can overcome barriers is to seek consultation from someone who is skilled in the application of the 3-5-7 Model©. When faced with challenges, workers often use more traditional methods to assist children and youth in the grieving process. The approach of the 3-5-7 Model© is different from traditional casework practices and requires a different way to view behaviors. To avoid "practice drift" from the 3-5-7 Model©, it is suggested that workers seek supervision from both peers and supervisors at regular intervals. Ask yourself or have a co-worker ask questions such as:

- In what context is the child/youth's behavior being interpreted?
- What stage of the grief cycle do the behaviors seem to be related to?
- How is the behavior informing the worker about what areas the child/youth needs to explore?
- What is the underlying feeling or question that the child/youth may be struggling with?
- Is the worker supporting the expression of feelings by lecturing and/or giving advice?
- Is the worker feeling pressured by caregivers to consequence behaviors as opposed to validating and being present to the expression?

In addition, reviewing the three tasks, five questions and seven skills when faced with barriers can assist a worker in responding to the child/youth in a way that supports the fidelity of the 3-5-7 Model©.

Resources

Beste, H.M. (1981). Developing a life story book program for foster children. *Child Welfare, 60* (8), 529-534.

Harrison, J., Campbell, E., & Chumbley, P. (2010). *Making history: A social worker's guide to lifebooks.* Frankfort, KY: Kentucky Cabinet for Health and Family Services.

Fahlberg, V. I. (1991). *A child's journey through placement.* Indianapolis, IN: Perspectives Press.

Henry, D.L. & Manning, G. (2011). Integrating child welfare and mental health practices: Actualizing youth permanency using the 3-5-7 Model. *Protecting Children*, 26 (1) 30-48.

Henry, D. L. (2010). *The 3-5-7 Model: A practice approach to permanency. Stories of hope & healing for children, youth and families.* Kearney, NE: Morris Publishing.

Henry, D. L. (2005). The 3-5-7 Model: Preparing children for permanency. *Children and Youth Services Review, 27*, 197-212.

Henry, D. (1999). Resilience in Maltreated Children Implications for Special Needs Adoption. *Child Welfare, 78* (5), 519-540.

Jewett, C.L. (1982). *Helping children cope with separation and loss.* Harvard, MA: The Harvard Common Press.

Keck, G.C. & Kupecky, R.M. (1995). *Adopting the hurt child.* Colorado Springs, CO: Pinion Press.

Keefer, B. & Schooler, J.E. (2000). *Telling the truth to your adopted or foster child: Making sense of the past.* Westport: Bergin & Garvey.

Leslie, K. (2004). *When a stranger calls you mom: A child development and relationship perspective on why abused and neglected children think, feel, and act the way they do.* Snow Camp, NC: Brand New Day Publishing.

Lewis, R.G. & Heffernan, M.S. (2000). *Adolescents & families for life: A tool kit for supervisors.*

Trozzi, M. (1999). *Talking with children about loss.* New York: Berkley Publishing.

Worden, J.W. (1996). *Children and grief: When a parent dies.* New York: The Guildford Press.

Helpful Websites

www.darlahenry.org
www.centerforloss.com

About the Authors

Stephanie Hodge Wolfe

Ms. Wolfe is a Licensed Social Worker and has a Bachelor's degree in Human Development and Family Studies from The Pennsylvania State University and a Master's degree in Social Work from The University of Pittsburgh. Ms. Wolfe lives and works in Pennsylvania, where she is a member of her local county Children's Roundtable, a group that works to address child permanency issues, and is also involved in her local county child welfare Permanency Practice Initiative Committee. Ms. Wolfe has been involved in child welfare practice in both the public and private sector for the past 15 years, with experience in a number of areas, including adoption, foster care and Family Group Decision Making. She was a contributor to Darla L. Henry's 2010 book, The **3-5-7 Model**©: A Practice Approach to Permanency, Stories of Hope & Healing for Children, Youth and Families.

Darla L. Henry

Darla L Henry is a Social Worker, Trainer, Teacher and Consultant having extensive experience in the Child Welfare field. With a mission to build a path toward healing and belongingness/permanency for children and youth in the child welfare system, Darla established and authored the **3-5-7 Model**©. This model is a practice approach for helping these children explore and tell their life stories towards resolution of the pain and hurt experienced from abusive/neglectful childhood experiences. The theories and components of this model support the activities of Family Finding and Family Group Decision Making as work that is done on the continuum of permanency options from reunification to adoption. Darla's doctoral research focused on **resilience** in maltreated children (Child Welfare, 1999) and provides the foundation for understanding the life experiences of children, youth and families who are engaged in child welfare services.

Her 40 years of working with public and private agencies, universities and governments have provided Darla with history and experience that guide her approaches to support and develop best practice programs that appeal to the hearts of workers and families who provide these permanency focused services. She has been honored to bring this message through workshops and consultations on the 3-5-7 Model© to many state programs: these include the California Permanency for Youth Project (13 rural and urban counties, including Los Angeles and San Francisco), as a follow up to Family Finding trainings by Kevin Campbell; New Hampshire DCFS (adopted as a statewide approach to permanency work); Wisconsin (Milwaukee training academy); and, conferences in Idaho, Florida, Connecticut, Ohio, and Arizona. As a former co-director of Family Design Resources, a prime contractor of the Pennsylvania Statewide Adoption and Permanency Network, Darla has been integral to the establishment and implementation of statewide Child Preparation services which contain components of the **3-5-7 Model**©.

Made in the USA
Middletown, DE
23 December 2016